MY CAT TOLD ME, MY DOG TOLD ME

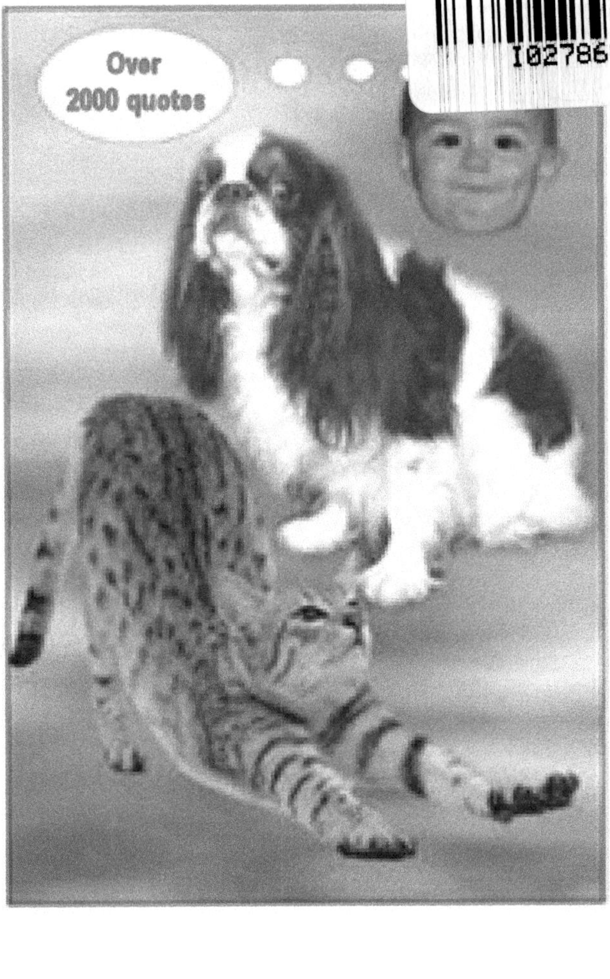

Over 2000 quotes

Didier HALLÉPÉE

Collection Animaux

MY CAT TOLD ME, MY DOG TOLD ME

Didier HALLÉPÉE

This book is sold subject to the condition that it shall not, by the way of trade or otherwise, be lent, resold, hired out, or otherwise circulated without the publisher's prior consent in any form of binding or cover other than that in which it is published and without a similar condition including this condition being imposed on the subsequent purchaser and without limiting the rights under copyright reserved above, no part of this publication may be reproduced, stored in or reproduced into a retrieval system or transmitted in any form or by any means (electronic, mechanical, photocopying, recording or otherwise), without the prior permission of both the copyright owner and the above-mentioned publisher of this book.

Copyright Didier Hallépée
2011

MY CAT TOLD ME, MY DOG TOLD ME

Didier HALLÉPÉE

Same author, Carrefour du Net publisher, paper books

"Le chat mau égyptien", 2009
"Citations et proverbes chats et chiens", 2009
"Mot à mau, les pensées du chat mau", 2010
"Pensées Royales Canines, les pensées du King Charles", 2010
"Les enfants du chat mau – histoire du chat de race", 2011
"Mon chat m'a dit, mon chien m'a dit", 2011

"L'univers de la monétique", 2009
"Le Sepa, l'espace des paiements en euro", 2009
"Qualité et sécurité informatique, les méthodes CMPI et CMSI", 2009
"La sécurité NFC", 2011
"La sécurité des systèmes embarqués", 2011

Same author, Carrefour du Net publisher, ebooks
"A ma fille", 2011
"Secrets de chat", 2011
"Secrets de chien", 2011
"Sudoku-neko volume 1", 2011
"Sudoku-neko volume 2", 2011
"Sudoku-neko volume 3", 2011
"Djambi, l'échiquier de Machiavel, *suivi du Sabacc*", 2011
"Le jeu de go", 2011
"Mon chat m'a conté", 2011
"Mon chien m'a conté", 2011
"Mon coq m'a conté", 2011
"Les secrets de Bastet, précis de génétique féline", 2011

Same author, Carrefour du Net publisher, in English
"The Egyptian Mau cat", 2011
"The Egyptian Mau children – story of the breed cat", 2011
"My cat told me, my dog told me", 2011
"Mau Mews (photo-comic)", 2011
"King Barks (photo-comic)", 2011
"Cat Secrets", 2011
"Dog Secrets", 2011
"Sudoku-neko volume 1", 2011
"Sudoku-neko volume 2", 2011
"Sudoku-neko volume 3", 2011
"CMPI, Managing and Mastering Computer Projects", 2009

Same author, Carrefour du Net publisher, in Italian
"I figli del gatto mau – storia del gatto di razza", 2011

to Isabelle, Leia and Jacen
with all my love.

Thanks to René Stouder, Patrick Le Coustumer and Zoran Radovanovic
for their help in the translation

Meet the author on his forum 'Fondcombe writers' http://forum.fondcombe.com

PREFACE

The cat and the dog have been occupying a prominent place in our homes and at our sides for many years. It is normal to come across them at any time in our literature or when visiting a website.

Sometimes they occupy the central place and there are many books that have been devoted to them, sometimes by writers less well known than their companions...

Other times, they are just making the scene more lively, more truthful, because without them, where would be the soul of our homes?

Out of context, some quotes retain their full flavor, others become dull. Not everyone spoke lovingly of their four-legged friends. Let them assume responsibility for what they said...

Through these quotes, you will first travel in time: Ancient India with Kautilya, the great strategist, Biblical times, the Egypt of pharaohs, the Middle-Age and modern times.

You will also travel across regions, countries and continents.

You will come upon famous names of our classical culture: Freud, Colette, Shakespeare, Einstein, Tacitus, Dumas, Cocteau and many others.

You will also discover what some celebrities may have said about cats: Elizabeth II, Obama, Sarkozy, Bouvard, Ruquier, Catherine Lara and many others.

Finally you'll find sentences from unknown people who will be remembered just because they liked dogs and cats.

This little journey into the heart of wisdom or in the company of famous personalities will give you all the delights that our fourlegged friends deserve.

And at the heart of all these treasures, I'm sure you will find valuable thoughts to illuminate your every day.

CAT, DOG AND MAN: THE LEGEND OF THE ORIGINS

Once upon a time, in another era, elves were travelling all over the world. They were said to be starfarers, refugees from a dying world who fled the dark evil lurking in the galaxies.

They had arrived during the age of the great dragons, those creatures whom we nowadays call dinosaurs. The great dragons' disappearance had reminded the elves that, immortal though they might be, they were not eternal, because even gods can accidentally die.

They had been living their bucolic way of life, filled with joy and songs, in the heart of the great impenetrable Sahara forest when the danger from outer space reappeared. Their hateful enemies had finally found them.

They had the appearance of gigantic wolves on whose faces one could read purely malevolent cruelty, a sort of cruelty which was not of this world! A magic cruelty ready to feast on the magic of the elves.

The confrontation was on a par with the magic powers which collided with each other! In the final battle magic destroyed magic, leaving only chaos and destruction in its wake. The Earth even shook on its orbit. The immense magnificent Sahara forest was destroyed forever, changed into a dry desert. Elves' songs would not soar from its foliage anymore.

Finally there came the time when the remaining handful of elves faced what was left of their enemies, the last remnants of the evil powers! Exhausted, worn out, the opponents had a break. Mutual extermination was close at hand. Neither of the two races could hope to prosper ever again. To grow and multiply had become a dream of the distant past, now forever unattainable. No stake whatsoever could justify this fight anymore.

Unable to win, the last survivors cast whatever was left of their magic powers in the final fight. Magic faced magic, one tragic and final time and so were destroyed the last remnants of magic in our world. So were destroyed absolute Evil and absolute Good too, leaving only Hope in our world!

And so were the last survivors of these two races deprived of their magic powers and so did they become mortal.

The elves became human! The noblest part in them was their longing for freedom which expressed itself in their communion with nature, in their supple wave-like gait, in that strange glance of theirs through green vertical pupils. Thus the essence of the elves became the cat! The essence of a freedom definitely lost to man and which would be the object of the aspirations most profoundly rooted in him!

The elves' enemies, for their part, lost much in size and power, savagery and cruelty, became wolves and dogs and lost their thirst for conquest and freedom. They swore loyalty to what remained of their former opponents.

Thus were born Man, Cat and Dog, and so was the place of each registered in heaven. Man would always dominate and aspire to freedom, a quest which would never satisfy him. The dog, in its staunch loyalty, couldn't even envision its lost freedom anymore. The cat, infatuated with freedom, would still look to man for its lost self but would never know rest. And cat and dog would forever keep within them part of the antagonism which had almost annihilated everything!

It's said that some were little affected by these transformations. Anubis told his own story, which was interpreted and passed on in the Book of the Dead. The last one of the race, so we are told, disappeared in France in the Gévaudan area.

Isis, Osiris, Seth and some others lived their last centuries in the heart of what used to be the impenetrable Sahara forest and which was soon going to become the deserts of Higher and Lower Egypt. Their narratives, badly understood by men, were going to turn them into the divinities of nascent Egypt.

The last one of them, Bastet, had kept both her humanity and her thirst for absolute freedom. Everything in her was expressed in her gait and feline look. She looked like a goddess with a cat's head and at the same time conveyed the bucolic sweetness of her race and the extremies of anger which had almost overcome their enemies.

And so Bastet the last survivor of these fantastic epics, became a goddess to these new people who could never again recover the magnificence of the elves from whom they descended. Bastet allowed the alliance of cats, her people, with human beings, allowing them to finally live side by side in a rough approximation of the unique being they once used to be. So man discovered that the cat was that part of the absolute which was missing in him.

It's said that some magic still lives in the most antique lineages of the cats of Egypt and that they can restore fragments of this lost past to a few chosen human beings.

Nowadays, the Egyptian Mau still carries in him the ancient blessing of Bastet. Conscious of this wealth, he expresses it through his noble look, his strong independent personality, his effusive tenderness for human beings. According to legend, the magic can be revived if and when one litter combines the four colors of the Mau: Silver, Bronze, Black Smoke and Black, - provided, of course, that their favorite human being proves to be worthy of them.

MY CAT TOLD ME

Inscriptions on the Royal Tombs at Thebes

Who is the Great Tomcat? He is the god Ra himself. He was called 'mau' when Sia spoke of him because he kept mewing all the time, and that was how his name as a cat came into being.

Thou art the Great Cat, the avenger of the Gods, and the judge of words, and the president of the sovereign chiefs and the governor of the Holy Circle; thou art indeed... the Great Cat.

Anonymous quotations

A cat can climb down from a tree without the assistance of the fire department or any other agency. The proof is, no one has ever seen a cat's skeleton in a tree.
Unknown

A cat has two left feet. However, there is no one so skilful!
Unknown

A cat is an example of sophistication minus civilization.
Unknown

A cat sees us as dogs... A cat sees himself as a human.
Unknown

A cat sleeps fat, yet walks thin.
Unknown

A cat will assume the shape of its container.
Unknown

A nice woman he has the man who loves cats.
Unknown

A thing of beauty, strength, and grace lies behind that whiskered face.
Unknown

Always look around when your cat gazes behind you with that intent look in her eyes. Some day there might actually be something there.
Unknown

An immobile cat still has open eyes.
Unknown

And if such a story has a moral, it surely must be that it is dangerous indeed to jump at conclusions.
Unknown

As he loves his cat, so he loves his wife.
Unknown

Cats have not been put on a pedestal, they get on to it themselves
Unknown

Cats are trying to teach us that in nature, not everything is required to have a role to play.
Unknown

Cats are experiments in consciousness with limited intelligence, humans are experiments in intelligence with limited consciousness.
Unknown

Cats understand our feelings. They don't care about them, but they understand them
Unknown

Civilization is defined by the presence of cats.
Unknown

Dogs bark, cats mew, but what do ants do?
Unknown

Every dog has his day – but nights belong to cats.
Unknown

Every life should have nine cats.
Unknown

With cats, the future belongs to those who lick themselves early.
Unknown

French novelist Colette was a firm cat-lover. When she was in the U.S. she saw a cat sitting in the street. She went over to talk to it and the two of them mewed at each other for a friendly minute. Colette turned to her companion and exclaimed, Enfin ! Someone who speaks French.
Unknown

God made the cat in order to give man the pleasure of caressing the tiger.
Unknown (ascribed to Victor Hugo, Joseph Méry, Rudyard Kipling)

Heaven will never be Heaven if my cats are not there to welcome me.
Unknown

How strange, how strange, how strange a tale! Look, a black cat with a tail.
Unknown

I figured we all started out as cats, but then the world put us on a leash and collar and turned us into dogs.
Unknown

I purr, therefore I am.
Unknown

If God created man in his own image, you've got to wonder in whose image did he create the cat, a more noble creature?
Unknown

If stretching meant wealth, the cat would be rich.

Unknown

If you want to know the character of a man, find out what his cat thinks of him.

Unknown

If you yell at a cat, you're the one who is making a fool of himself.

Unknown

In every cat there lies a guardian angel.

Unknown

In Paris during the winter solstice, the French are used to building a huge bonfire and place on top of it a cage in which they lock up a fox and two dozen cats before setting it on fire. They say King Francis does not consider it beneath him setting the cage on fire himself.

Unknown

In the eyes of cats, all things belong to them.

Unknown

It's in cat trees that you find kittens.

Unknown

It's really the cat's house - we are content to pay the rent.

Unknown

It's very hard to be polite if you're a cat.

Unknown

It wasn't curiosity that killed the cat; I did it with the lawnmower.

Unknown

My cat was bought in a ketchup.

Unknown

My husband said it was either him or the cat...I miss him sometimes.

Unknown

My little grandson is a darling, but he'll never take the place of my cats.

Unknown

On the eighth day God created the Cat.

Unknown

Once upon a time a cat who prided herself on her wit and wisdom was prowling about the barn in search of food and saw a tail protruding from a hole. This is the appendage of a rat, she said to herself. Then she crept stealthily towards it and when she was within striking distance she made a jump at it and grasped it with her claws. Alas! It was not the appendage of

a rat, but the tail of a snake, who whisked round and gave her a mortal bite.
Unknown

Purring is an automatic safety-valve device for dealing with excess of happiness.
Unknown

Rat got my tongue, said the Angora cat.
Unknown

Researchers have discovered that dogs can comprehend a vocabulary of 2,000 words, whereas cats can only comprehend 25 to 50. No one ever asked themselves how many words researchers can comprehend.
Unknown

Some people own cats and go on leading normal lives.
Unknown

The cat is mightily dignified until the dog comes along.
Unknown

The purity of a person's heart can be quickly assessed by the way he or she regards cats.
Unknown

There are many intelligent species in the universe. All are owned by cats.
Unknown

There is no snooze button on a cat who wants breakfast.
Unknown

Woman, cat and dog have fleas all along the year.
Unknown

Woman's knee, dog's nose, cat's paw: has there ever been anything so cold?
Unknown

Read our illustrated quotations in

Mot à mau
Mau Mews
Didier Hallépée
Carrefour du Net publisher

bilingual edition

Quotations from authors

A real gentleman is the one who always calls a spade a spade, even if he stumbles on a cat and falls over.
Marcel Achard

His voice sounded like that of a cat trying to get her claws into a piece of nylon.
Douglas Adams

_ How do you know he exists? How do you know that you look nice to him?
_ I don't know. Simply, it makes me happy to have a definite attitude towards what seems to me to be a cat.
Douglas Adams

I think all cats are wild. They act tamely only if there's a saucer of milk waiting for them.
Douglas Adams

He left very dignified and stiff, with concentrated air, furtive eyes and perplexed brows, like a leopard not quite sure he saw a half empty box of wet food for cats lying abandoned five hundred yards ahead of him on a hot and dusty plain.
Douglas Adams

If you try and take a cat apart to see how it works, the first thing you have got on your hands is a non-working cat.
Douglas Adams

Siamese Cats have a way of their own of staring at you. Those who have walked in on the Queen cleaning her teeth will know the expression.
Douglas Adams

There is more fun at the bottom of a cat litter.
Douglas Adams

Managers are like cats in a litter box. They instinctively shuffle things around to conceal what they've done.
Scott Adams

When the marmot plays or you caress it, its voice sounds like the murmur of a small dog or the purr of a cat.
Michel Adanson

A cat comes up when you call her - if she doesn't have anything better to do.
Bill Adler

In Egypt, cats... afford evidence that animal nature is not altogether intractable but that, when well-treated, animals are good at remembering kindness.
Aelian

The cat does not make you impure nor does it sully your water for ablutions.
Aisha, the wife of the Prophet

Cats are successful underachievers. They only need to purr in order to get free food and TLC. What other creature can lie around the house doing nothing beyond purring, and still get free food and TLC?
Jim Aites

There is no man for man: we are lying in wait for each other, like the cat for the mouse.
Mateo Aleman

Raton has nothing to fear for his paws, and there is no such fuss about the little trick he has done.
Jean le Rond d'Alembert

If the pull of the outside world is strong, there is also a pull towards the human. The cat may disappear on its own errands, but sooner or later, it returns once again for a little while, to greet us with its own type of love. Independent as they are, cats find more than pleasure in our company.
Lloyd Alexander

Most cats do not approach humans recklessly. The possibility of concealed weapons, clods or sticks, tend to make them reserved. Homeless cats in particular--with some justification, unfortunately--consider humans their natural enemies. Much ceremony must be observed and a number of diplomatic feelers put out, before establishing a state of truce.
Lloyd Alexander

The cat liked to peep into the refrigerator and risked having his head caught by the closing door. He also climbed on to the top of the stove, discontinuing the practice after he singed his tail.
Lloyd Alexander

Two cats can live as cheaply as one, and their owner has twice as much fun.
Lloyd Alexander

When you see a cat's paw lightly wash his pink nose and smooth his hair so fine, then fraternally embrace this feline.
Alphonse Allais

In the midst of a world that has always been a bit mad, the cat walks about with confidence.
Rosanne Amberson

As anyone who has been with a cat for any length of time well knows, cats have enormous patience with the limitations of the human mind. They realize... that we have an infuriating inability to understand, let alone follow, even the simplest and most explicit of directions.
Cleveland Amory

One of the ways in which cats show happiness is by sleeping.
Cleveland Amory

And the cat said:
– Can you arch your back, or purr?
– No
– So, don't express absurd opinions when sensible people are talking.
Andersen

Do not laugh at a cat.
Ankhsheshonq

When a man smells of myrrh, his wife is a kitten to him.
When a man is suffering, his wife is a lioness to him.
Ankhsheshonq

A cat killed without any real desire.
It was a very rich cat and was not really hungry.
Jean Anouilh

I want in my house
A woman with her reason,
A cat weaving among books,
Friends in all seasons
Whom I cannot live without.
Guillaume Apollinaire

Some see "God" as "dog" spelled backwards. I see "God" as "cat" spelled with a vivid imagination.
Jacob Appel

The Siamese cat leapt silently and rubbed against one of the bare feet.
Louis Aragon

Despite his impatience to have his dream come true, he didn't leave the house until he had checked that his one-eyed, three-legged cat was sound asleep on the kitchen boiler. [...] The first thing he did on returning was to feed the cat.
Jeffrey Archer

If he had one regret at all, it was that he hadn't been able to bring his ginger cat with him.
Jeffrey Archer

Female cats are very lascivious and make advances to male cats.
Aristote

*The Dog and the Cat.
An open foe I much prefer
To a dear friend that scratches.*
Arnadlt

Doc, there were four rats in this cage when I changed my bulbs. And now there are only three. Upon reflection, I think rat n° 4 must be located inside this cat.
Jack Arnold

When my teeth are not threatened, all the cats in the world are not dangerous.
Antonin Artaud

Indifferent to his past, careless of his future, the cat that has nine lives, more or less, has naturally increased in numbers despite the abuse he has suffered.
Yann Arthus-Bertrand

The cat sleeps on the sheik's lap and is at home on the prayer carpet.
Attar

Cats can be very funny, and have the oddest ways of showing they're glad to see you. Rudimac always peed in our shoes.
W. H. Auden

*_ I love dogs.
_ Well then, if you love dogs, why don't you have one?
_ Because my wife doesn't like them, she prefers cats.
_ Do you have a cat?
_ No. It's dirty. My wife wants a cat that won't be dirty.
_ A cat is less dirty than a dog.
_ What 's more dirty is canaries. My wife didn't want any either, but then I stamped my foot. Yes, I did.*
Michel Audiard

When I wake my cat up, he seems as grateful as one who is given the opportunity to sleep again.
Michel Audiard

At dusk, to dogs and wolves, all cats are grey.
Yvan Audouard

You dare to ask me who have a dog, a cat, a turtle, two children, a wife and several mothers-in-law if I love animals?!
Yvan Audouard

Dear friends, we've had our share of sorrow and joy this year. Troubles first. Our little cat Snowball was run over by a car. He went to kitty paradise. But we bought a new little cat, Snowball II, life goes on.
Véronique Augereau

We could see all around the stories of the most famous cats: Robillardus hung upside down on the board of rats, Puss- in- Boots Marquis de Carabas, the Cat who writes, the Cat who became a woman, the witches who became cats, the Sabbath and all its ceremonies.
Madame d'Aulnoy

Life is life - whether in a cat, a dog or man. There is no difference there between a cat and a man. The idea of such a difference is man's conception - to his own advantage.
Sri Aurobindo

Concerning an incomprehensible poem or a finely insignificant novel, he usually said that it was mush for cats.
Marcel Aymé

A cat will never drown if she sees the shore.
Francis Bacon

After her children have married, a mother occupies herself with raising cats.
Ahmad Bahgat

I remember that in my early childhood I used to fast, and whenever fasting was over I would go out taking my meal with me and give it to the stray dogs and cats.
Ahmad Bahgat

When cats aren't in, mice can dance.
Jean Antoine de Baïf

A cat's hearing apparatus is such that it allows the human voice to easily go in at one ear and out at the other.
Stephen Baker

Cats are notoriously sore losers. Coming in second best, especially to someone as poorly coordinated as a human being, grates on their feelings.
Stephen Baker

Most beds sleep up to six cats. Even ten cats - without the owner.
Stephen Baker

Kittens are born with their eyes shut. They open them about six days later, take a look around, then close them again for the better part of their lives.
Stephen Baker

By dint of being whipped, I realized that external cleanliness should be under an English Pussy.
Honoré de Balzac

Sky is in her eyes, hell is in her heart.
Honoré de Balzac

The tail of our ancestors' cats was wide, high and thick.
Honoré de Balzac

The most beautiful cats' privilege is to run off with the grace that distinguishes you and to go who knows where, to give themselves a lick.
Honoré de Balzac

A dog, a cat is a heart with hair around.
Brigitte Bardot

I prefer the company of animals to that of humans.
Brigitte Bardot

If God is everywhere, the door that opens onto him is everywhere: the rose, the little cat, the morning stars. But the door closest to man is man.
René Barjavel

_ My name is Smokey, said the cat.
_ This is not a name, I'll call you Gri-Gri...
_ As you wish. Anyway, I never come when I'm called.
René Barjavel

As the English say, curiosity killed the cat.
Carl Barks

Good curiosity probably saved many cats.
Carl Barks

Surely the cat, when it assumes the meat loaf position and gazes meditatively through slitted eyes, is pondering thoughts of utter profundity...

Dogs have owners, cats have staff.

Mij Colson Barnum

If I die before my cat, I want a I few of my ashes put in his food so I can live inside him.

Dave Barry

A cat is a free being. And ever so full of love. It's hard not to envy a cat.

Drew Barrymore

There's no need for a piece of sculpture in a home that has a cat.

Henri Bates

Breeding purebred cats is like searching for perfection

Wesley Bates

And particles of gold, like fine grains of sand,
dimly spangle their mystic eyes.

Melissa Bateson

Both ardent lovers and austere scholars
Love in their mature years
The strong and gentle cats, pride of the house,
Who, like them, are sedentary and sensitive to cold.

Charles Baudelaire

The Cat is beautiful, it arouses ideas of luxury, cleanliness, and voluptuousness.

Charles Baudelaire

Chinese read time in cats' eyes.

Charles Baudelaire

I see with amazement
The fire of his pale pupils,
Clear signal-lights, living opals,
That contemplate me fixedly.

Charles Baudelaire

In my mind wanders,
As in his apartment
A beautiful cat, strong, sweet and charming.
When it mews, you can barely hear it.

Charles Baudelaire

As if at the feet of a queen, a voluptuous cat.

Charles Baudelaire

The child is unruly, selfish, devoid of gentleness and patience, and cannot serve as a confidant to lonely pains. A pure animal can, such as a dog or a cat.
Charles Baudelaire

Come, superb cat, to my amorous heart;
Hold back the talons of your paws,
Let me gaze into your beautiful eyes
Of metal and agate.
Charles Baudelaire

When they dream, they assume the noble attitudes
Of the mighty sphinxes stretched out in solitude,
Who seem to fall into a sleep of endless dreams.
Charles Baudelaire

The majority of people who still have back doors don't let their cats go out or come in through them.
Charlene Beane

_ I imagine myself on a deserted island with a guitar, two women and three cats.
_ Shocking! More cats than women!
Guy Béart & Jade

Wilt thou, my Rosinette
Go shopping
For the King of husbands?
I'm not Tircis;
But in the shade of night,
I am still worth my price
And when it is dark
The most beautiful cats are gray.
Beaumarchais

Sorry, excuse me, she said, I can't find the concierge. It's for cutting a cat.
Simone de Beauvoir

To some extent, a cat could be another me or, better, a master model.
Béatrix Beck

Any household with at least one feline member has no need for an alarm clock.
Louise A. Belcher

*Belaud, I promise you, in good faith,
That you shall live as long on Earth
as Cats war against Rats.*

Joachim du Bellay

*Small nose, small teeth
Eyes that were not too eager
But where the blue pupil
Imitates the various color
Seen in this rainbow
that curves through the sky.*

Joachim du Bellay

The cat is Parisian, the cat is a senior executive, the cat looks at Ségolène, the cat is bobo, the cat is Libé.

Zysla Belliat

You are my cat and I am your human.

Hilaire Belloc

I think it rather fine, this necessity for the tense bracing of the will before anything worth doing can be done. I rather like it myself. I feel it to be the chief thing that differentiates me from the cat by the fire.

Arnold Bennett

Happiness is like a cat, if you try to coax it or call it, it will avoid you; it will never come. But if you pay no attention to it and go about your business, you'll find it rubbing against your legs and jumping into your lap.

William John Bennett

A Swiss guard, smiling, said, «My Eminence, see, cats mount an assault on the holy seat."
To which Ratzinger replied "oh it does not seem that they are really so dangerous."

Benedict XVI

He lives in half light, in secret places, free and alone - this mysterious little great being whom his mistress calls 'My cat.'

Margaret Benson

The cat is, above all things, a dramatist.

Margaret Benson

In the golden eyes of the cat and the deep sweet brown ones of the Setter, there was all the tenderness of the world.

Juliette Benzoni

Hardly had she found her bed than she curled into a ball like a cat and without even thinking of undressing slept like a log, with her head in his arms.
Juliette Benzoni

As every cat owner knows, nobody owns a cat.
Ellen Perry Berkeley

Richelieu was not that unpleasant. He loved cats.
Stéphane Bern

He (Benedict XVI) speaks with them, neither in German nor Italian, but using a particular and transcendent language and the felines who listen charm him.
Monseigneur Bertone

Cats, small or big, are perhaps the most beautiful creatures on this earth.
Claire Bessant

Well, says Love hiding in paradox, what is a lover? It is an instrument which is rubbed to have fun. Cuvier said to me: "Your cat does not caress you, it caresses itself against you."
Henri Beyle (Stendhal)

Purring is the cat's smile.
Hector Bianciotti

Cat: A soft, indestructible automaton provided by nature to be kicked when things go wrong in the domestic circle.
Ambrose Bierce

Violin: An instrument to tickle human ears by friction of a horse's tail on the entrails of a cat.
Ambrose Bierce

Sacred, adj. Dedicated to some religious purpose; having a divine character; inspiring solemn thoughts or emotions; such as... the Cow in India; the Crocodile, the Cat and the Onion of ancient Egypt.
Ambrose Bierce

I called my cat William because no shorter name fits the dignity of his character. Poor old boy, he has fits now, so I call him Fitz-William.
Josh Billings

At the peak of heat in summer months, [...] the cat remains dry and cold. A cat will not stay with a man, except the one who feeds him.
Hildegarde de Bingen

Grief is a kind of wild cat, grey in colour. His cry is rather sad and gloomy.
Francis Blanche

Better feed one's mind than Siamese cats.

Francis Blanche

A dog will make eye contact. A cat will, too, but a cat's eyes don't even look entirely warm-blooded to me, whereas a dog's eyes look human, though less guarded. A dog will look at you as if to say, "What do you want me to do for you? I'll do anything for you." Whether a dog can, in fact, do anything for you if you don't have sheep (I never have) is another matter. The dog is willing to help.

Roy Blount Jr.

Cats have brushed against my ankle on crossing my way for so long that my gait, both at home and out of doors, has been compared to that of a man wading through low surf.

Roy Blount, Jr.

I do not know what the cat may have been eating. Usually I know exactly what the cat has eaten. Not only have I fed it to the cat, at the cat's insistence, but the cat has thrown it up on the rug, and someone has tracked it on to the other rug. I do not know why cats are such habitual vomiters. They do not seem to enjoy it, judging by the sounds they make while doing it. It's their nature. A dog will bark. A cat will vomit.

Roy Blount Jr.

If a cat spoke, it would say things like, 'Hey, I don't see what's the problem here'.

Roy Blount, Jr.

Dogs come when they're called. Cats take the message and call you back.

Mary Bly

A Mouse is afraid of cats, a cat is afraid of dogs.

Christian Bobin

Thus, there are people who free you from yourself as naturally as does the sight of a cherry blossom or a kitten playing at catching its tail. These people's real work is their presence.

Christian Bobin

To keep a proper perspective of one's own importance, everyone should have a dog who adores him and a cat who ignores him.

Christian Bobin

Cats' love is the first step towards aesthetics.

Isabelle Bonte

The name of the god who guards you is Cat.

The Book of the Dead

Who Is This Cat?
This cat is Ra himself, and he was called 'Mau' because of the words of god Sa concerning him: 'He is like light (Mau) out which he was made; therefore did the name of Ra become 'Mau'.
The Book of the Dead

A man who was loved by 300 women singled me out to live with him. Why? I was the only one without a cat.
Elayne Boosler

He is a cat, therefore he is free.
Gilbert Bordes

Our cats live in the company of dogs, ferrets and other cats of the house. They spend their day eating, sleeping, climbing all over the place, hunting mice (toys)... Their schedule is overbusy. At the age of three months, they know the taboos from other occupants of the house (curtains, kitchen table, living room table, dog bed...)
Bernard Boucher

They fear that some beings more powerful than themselves - dogs or humans – could cause them some damage or some injury.
Mikhaïl Boulgakov

Animals were created by God to give men a sense of superiority.
Philippe Bouvard

Cats are creatures that express a multitude of moods and attitudes.
Karen Brademeyer

If you are too gentle with a cat who lives with you, he looks like fanning himself and has a distant look, like those bitches of yore who seemed to say: Come on, speak by all means, I'm not concerned.
Pierre Brasseur

Adopted in Japan by the imperial family at the end of the first millennium, the cat became the ancestor of Maneki Neko, a small white cat statuette sitting with one leg lifted, which is found in much of Asia where it is a sign of happiness.
Raymonde Branger

At dinner time he would sit in a corner, concentrating, and suddenly they would say, 'Time to feed the cat,' as if it were his own idea.
Lilian Jackson Braun

Cats never strike a pose that isn't photogenic.
Lillian Jackson Braun

To understand a cat, you must realize that he has his own gifts, his own viewpoint, even his own morality.

Lilian Jackson Braun

When George in Pudding time came o'er,
And Moderate Men looked big, Sir,
My Principles I chang'd once more,
And so became a Whig, Sir.

Vicar of Bray

It is a cat of ill fortune
A poor alley cat
Having tamed me
He did not teach me
only good manners
so as to be a good cat.

Marcel Bréchet

The little cat is dead, Sunday Muscal does not make them sing anymore.

Jacques Brel

We brought with us a cat in the ship, a most amicable cat and greatly loved by us; but he grew to a monstrous size through the eating of fish.

St Brendan

We'll have one day to make up our minds and call a spade a spade and bus stoning an act of urban terrorism.

Alexis Brezet

A cat isn't fussy--just so long as you remember he likes his milk in the shallow, rose-patterned saucer and his fish on the blue plate. From which he will pick it, and eat it off the floor.

Arthur Bridges

Cats have an infallible understanding of total concentration--and get between you and it.

Arthur Bridges

It was love at first sight, he looked at you, the current passed, it was he and no other.

Alyse Brisson

The aim of a cat breeder is perfection.

Alyse Brisson

The statuesque Egyptian Mau silhouetted in the evening dusk quickly transports you to the pyramids of ancient Egypt.

Dot Brocksom

I can say with sincerity that I love cats. A cat is an animal that has more human feelings than anyone else.
Emilie Brontë

A cat is nobody's fool.
Heywood Brown

A cat can maintain a position of curled up somnolence in your lap until you are nearly upright. At the last minute she hopes your conscience will get the better of you and you will sit down again.
Pam Brown

Cats can work out mathematically exactly where to sit so as to cause most inconvenience.
Pam Brown

Seen from a distance, cats are beautiful. Close up they are a thing of incomparable splendor. In all their actions is perfection.
Pam Brown

Many a cat can only be lured in by switching off all the lights and keeping very still. Until the indignant cry of a locked-out cat can be heard outside the door.
Pam Brown

One small cat changes coming home to an empty house into Coming Home.
Pam Brown

The trouble with sharing one's bed with cats is that they'd rather sleep on you than beside you.
Pam Brown

Places where to look: behind the books in the bookshelf, in any cupboard with a gap too small for any cat to squeeze through, at the top of anything beyond reach, under anything too low for a cat to squeeze under and inside the piano.
Roseanne Ambrose-Brown

The cat has been described as the most perfect animal, the acme of muscular perfection and the supreme example in the animal kingdom of the coordination of mind and muscle.
Roseanne Ambrose Brown

In order to keep a true perspective of one's importance, everyone should have a dog that will worship him and a cat that will ignore him.
Dereke Bruce

The reason cats are such climbers is that they can look down on almost every other animal... it's also the reason they hate birds.
KC Buffington

When you are looking at it, a cat acts like a princess, but the very minute it thinks you are not looking, a cat acts like a fool.
KC Buffington

Nothing on earth could keep any cats a moment longer in a place where they would not want to be.
Georges Louis Leclerc, comte de Buffon

The cat is beautiful, light, clever, clean and sensual.
Georges Louis Leclerc, comte de Buffon

The cat is the only animal which accepts comfort but rejects the bondage of domesticity.
Georges Louis Leclerc, comte de Buffon

The cat is an unfaithful servant that one keeps only by sheer necessity.
Georges Louis Leclerc, comte de Buffon

Prowling about his own quiet backyard or lying asleep by the fire, he is still only a whisker away from the wilds.
Jean Burden

I love cats. I even think we have one at home.
Edward L Burlingame

Hatred of the cat reflects a spirit ugly, stupid, boorish, bigoted.
William Seward Burroughs

The cat does not offer services. The cat offers itself. Of course he wants care and shelter. You don't buy love for nothing. Like all pure creatures, cats are practical.
William Seward Burroughs

The message of the cauda equina is that either you're driving a cement mixer or doing the kitty litter and neither one nor the other inspires an erection.
Gérard Butler

I must have a cat whom I 'll find homeless, wandering about the courtyard, and to whom, therefore, I will be under no obligation. I have already selected a dirty little drunken wretch of a kitten to be the successor to my poor old cat.
Samuel Butler

If we treated everyone we meet with the same affection we bestow upon our favourite cat, they, too, would purr.
Martin Buxbaum

To err is human, to purr is feline.
Robert Byrne

Grand Duduche: "I am an animal lover... "
The Black Cat: "But I'm not a lover of mankind!
Cabu

Personally, I would not give a fig for any man's religion from which horse, cat and dog would not draw any benefits. Life in any form is our perpetual responsibility.
S. Parkes Cadman

Her name means "cat" and "light" in Egyptian. Descending probably from a subspecies of spotted African wild cats, our superb Mau was domesticated in ancient Egypt and was made the object of true worship. The Egyptians used her in their fight against rodents in which she was found to be more effective than weasels, the Greeks are supposed to have "robbed" Maus for this very reason!
Christelle Cailleux

Impossible not to mention, almost in spite of oneself, the little cat who sleeps at the light junction of these lines of lingerie.
Louis Calaferte

She had a swan's neck, a cat's eyes, an eagle's gaze, a wasp's waist, a gazelle's legs, a lion's temperament, a dog's character. Yet, she was a woman.
Louis Calaferte

It was the heart of summer when, on hot rooftops, cats were making love to their females trembling like women. Love with cries of love.
Henri Calet

The city of cats and the city of men exist one inside the other, but they are not the same city.
Italo Calvino

When the barometer washes itself behind its ears, the cat forecasts rain.
Léo Campion

The cats raised their eyes pale with sleep, without yet stirring
Albert Camus

A cat determined not to be found can fold itself up like a pocket handkerchief if it wants to.

Louis Camuti

Cat people are different to the extent that they generally are non-conformists. How could they be otherwise with a cat running their lives?

Louis Camuti

When out, most cats want to be in, and vice versa, and often simultaneously.

Louis Camuti

With dogs and people, it's love in big splashy colors. When you're involved with a cat, you're dealing in pastels.

Louis Camuti

Cats are a tonic, they are a laugh, they are a cuddle, they are at least pretty just about all of the time and beautiful some of the time.

Roger A. Caras

Cats can be cooperative when something feels good, which, to a cat, is the way everything is supposed to feel as often as possible.

Roger A. Caras

Cats don't like change without their consent.

Roger A. Caras

Cats fear water, so they prefer sunbathing.

Stéphane Caron

In every kennel there sleeps a dog.

Gilles Carrez

Bless their little pointed faces and their big, loyal, loving hearts. If a cat did not put a firm paw down now and then, how could his human remain in his possession?

Winifred Carriere

Cats always know whether people like or dislike them. They do not always care enough to do anything about it.

Winifred Carriere

The dog growls when it's angry and wags its tail when happy. I growl when I'm pleased and wag my tail when I am angry. So I'm mad! (Cheshire cat).

Lewis Carroll

It is a very inconvenient habit of kittens (Alice had once made the remark) that whatever you say to them, they always purr.

Lewis Carroll

'Would you tell me, please, which way I ought to go from here?'
'That depends a good deal on where you want to get to,' said the Cat.
'I don't much care where - ' said Alice.
'Then it doesn't matter which way you go,' said the Cat.
' - so long as I get somewhere,' Alice added as an explanation.
'Oh, you're sure to do that,' said the Cat, 'if you only walk long enough'.
Lewis Carroll

In the Middle Ages, cats and cat women were regarded as evil. Nonsense, of course, witches were just single, independent women who broke society's rules
Catwoman

Legend has it that priestesses became the first catwomen ever. The cats they'd worshipped –Midnight's ancestors –gave up each one of their nine lives to bring them back from the dead.
Catwoman

Those who will play with cats must expect to be scratched.
Miguel de Cervantes

A kitten is the delight of the household; all day long a comedy is played out by an incomparable actor.
Jules Champfleury (Jules Husson)

A drowsing little cat is an image of perfect beatitude.
Jules Champfleury (Jules Husson)

If you would know what a cat is thinking about, you must hold its paw in your hand for a long time.
Jules Champfleury (Jules Husson)

Nothing is so difficult as to paint the cat's face, which as Moncrif justly observes, bears a character of finesse and hilarity. The lines are so delicate, the eyes so strange, the movements subject to such sudden impulses, that one should be feline oneself to portray such a subject.
Jules Champfleury (Jules Husson)

There is no more intrepid explorer than a kitten.
Jules Champfleury (Jules Husson)

Do not think he caresses you, he caresses himself.
Chamfort

Of all domestic animals the cat is the most expressive. His face is capable of showing a wide range of expressions. His tail is a mirror of his mind. His gracefulness is surpassed only by his agility. And, along with all this, he has a sense of humor.

Walter Chandoha

Old ma Michel lost her cat
[...]
Your cat will be sold as a rabbit!
Chanson

An animal never takes back the love it gives you.
Madeleine Chapsal

Nothing is sadder than to see people unhappy with themselves and everything, who tickle each other to set each other laughing.
Emile-Auguste Chartier (Alain)

Two things are aesthetically perfect in the world - the clock and the cat.
Emile-Auguste Chartier (Alain)

There is something of the camel about cats
R. Chartrand

The cat lives alone, has no need for companionship, obeys only when he feels like it, pretends to be asleep to see things more clearly, and scratches everything on which he can put his paw.
François René, vicomte de Chateaubriand

What I like in the cat is this independent almost ungrateful character that makes him focus on nobody, and the indifference with which he can go from living rooms to native alleys.
François René, vicomte de Chateaubriand

Cat year (Chinese horoscope)

This is New Year
Cat, mother cat, kitten, warmth
Of a family.
Alexandre Chatelain

Let take a cat, and fostre him wel with milk, And tendre flesh, and make his couche of silk, And let him seen a mous go by the wal; Anon he weyveth milk, and flesh, and al, And every deyntee that is in that hous, Swich appetyt hath he to ete a mous.
Geoffrey Chaucer

But nature does not say that cats are more valuable than mice; nature makes no remark on the subject. She does not even say that the cat is enviable or the mouse pitiable. We think the cat superior because we have (or most of us have) a particular philosophy to the effect that life is better than death. But if the mouse were a German pessimist mouse, he

might not think that the cat had beaten him at all. He might think he had beaten the cat by getting to the grave first.
Gilbert Keith Chesterton

Someone really superstitious is one who is convinced that passing under a black cat brings bad luck.
Jean-Loup Chiflet

I hate you, your house smells of cat piss! Why do all the houses of drug dealers smell of cat piss?
Margaret Cho

A child turns his desire into action without the slightest scruple. If he is angry against his cat, he will say "I'll kill you", and he will strike him on the head with a hammer. Then he will have a broken heart because his cat does not come back to life.
Agatha Christie

A green emerald because I was a mysterious cat with green eyes
Agatha Christie

A green light shone in her eyes. Eyes that looked like a cat's.
Agatha Christie

A mother cannot declare that she no longer wants her children and abandon them just like that. Or eat them. As she- cats do when they have too many kittens.
Agatha Christie

All she wants is to be allowed to curl up and purr.
Agatha Christie

Damn cats! they ravage my flower beds and I can't stand hearing them mew.
Agatha Christie

Felines obey rules laid down precisely by them. In the same way that your cats congregate around my friend who hates them, they pay no attention to me who don't stop making advances.
Agatha Christie

For a brief moment, I thought I saw a cat paw in his hand and his outstretched arm, and in his voice, I thought I perceived a purr.
Agatha Christie

He had survived the most powerful hurricane that hit Jamaica. What most marked them, he and his parents, was seeing their cat running about like a madman all over the house.
Agatha Christie

He had that gleam in the eye, well known to his colleagues, which was reminiscent of cats.

Agatha Christie

He is like a cat. And cats are thieves.

Agatha Christie

He looked like a cat attentive to a flock of chirping birds and to their comings and goings. But the cat was not yet ready to pounce.

Agatha Christie

Her reddish-blond hair in a bun and Katherine being her last name earned her "Sandy Cat" as a nickname.

Agatha Christie

I do not know who invented curiosity. It is usually attributed to cats. Curious as an old cat.

Agatha Christie

I live for my cats. They are my only joy, my only pleasure in life. I do my utmost for them.

Agatha Christie

I never met a man with eyes as green as a cat's.

Agatha Christie

I remember the smell of white dust in the courtyard of the stables, the red cat who wandered gravely, the scraping of horses' hooves on the floor of their stall.

Agatha Christie

I was the cat watching the mouse, the dog smelling his scent without ever losing it. And the squirrel too. Now, I'll look in my reserve for some nuts I put aside long ago.

Agatha Christie

It is so difficult to know what's part of the carpet and what's part of the cat's tail.

Agatha Christie

It sounded deep and full, like the ecstatic purring of a cat.

Agatha Christie

It was a nasty brat and a brute! He kept torturing cats and strays and bullying his classmates.

Agatha Christie

It was not conscious cruelty. His conduct was as natural and instinctive as the cat playing with a mouse.

Agatha Christie

Just think of any normal cat. She has her kittens, she shows passionately protective of them and she scratches all those who approach them. And then, after a week or two, she begins to have a life of her own. She goes, she hunts a bit, she rests from her litter. She continues to protect her offspring if anyone attacks them, but they cease to obsess her constantly. She also plays a little with them. But they are a little too excited, she gets angry and administers a good spanking, and she tells them she wants a moment alone. It comes back, you see, her nature. As they grow up, she cares less and less about them. Her thoughts turn to the attractive neighborhood tomcats. This is what might be regarded as the normal pattern of existence of the female sex.

Agatha Christie

Let me see... You've recently talked to a Spaniel, my little finger tells me. The dogs here are idiots if you ask me. What's that? A cat? That's interesting! Too bad he is not here. He would have provided a nice hunt. Hmm... Not bad, this bull terrier.

Agatha Christie

Only cats and witches roam by night.

Agatha Christie

She is hypersensitive. Like those people who feel that there is a cat in the room long before seeing it.

Agatha Christie

She loved comfort, like cats love cream.

Agatha Christie

She never ceases to open and close her hands like a cat making his claws.

Agatha Christie

She reminds me of a cat, a fat lazy purring cat... I have nothing against cats, mind you. I do not blame cats, but...

Agatha Christie

She was licking her chops like a cat who had found a bowl of cream. She would nearly have purred with satisfaction!

Agatha Christie

The beautiful grey Persian who sat on his knees looked up at him with ecstasy; he began to knead the thigh and plunged suddenly his claws in it as if it were a ball where it was appropriate to plant his pins.

Agatha Christie

The red cat was still perched on the gate of the villa. Sitting upright, he had finally stopped washing his nose with his paw and was gently swaying tail, dominating the assembly with that disdain for the human race, which is the prerogative of camels and cats.
Agatha Christie

Then he realized that the red fur neck-lace was a cat. Three other cats rippled in the hallway, two of them mewing furiously. They t glared at visitors, turning slowly around the skirts of their mistress. A strong smell of cat offended the nostrils.
Agatha Christie

There is definitely a needle somewhere in the haystack and among the cats that sleep there, one there is that I will wake up.
Agatha Christie

These cats are rational animals, at least if you behave reasonably with them.
Agatha Christie

They use guinea pigs, I think... It is cruel... but less than dogs, of course... or even cats.
Agatha Christie

There is this cat-like streak about us, women… mew, mew, scratch scratch, purr purr…
Agatha Christie

Two brats amused themselves by torturing a cat. As she approached to remonstrate with them, the cat resolutely used its claws and succeeded in escaping.
Agatha Christie

Unfortunately for him, he belonged to that category of human beings who cannot see cats in painting. As always in these cases, the cats ran in troops. One of them jumped on to his lap while another rubbed affectionately against his pant legs.
Agatha Christie

What if we discover that we both love dogs and cats and that we hate red. This is what is called a "common thread" between us.
Agatha Christie

What's that? A cat? That's interesting! Too bad he's not here. He would have provided a nice hunt.
Agatha Christie

When the cat is there, the little mouse does not approach the cheese.

> Agatha Christie

When the cat plays with a mouse, he follows his instinct. Nature is like that.

> Agatha Christie

All dogs look up to you. All cats look down on you. Only the pig looks at you as an equal.

> Winston Churchill

*The Cat goes out
And the cat comes back
And no one can follow her
Upon her track.
She knows where she's going
She knows where she's been, all we can do
Is to let her in.*

> Marchette Chute

*On a dressing table
This cat saw a mirror.
He jumps, looks and at first thinks
He sees one of his brothers watching.*

> Jean-Pierre Claris de Florian

Even the stupidest cat seems to know more than any dog.

> Eleanor Clark

Every cat is special in its own way.

> Sara Jane Clark

He caressed her and immediately she began to purr. He felt the vibration, he heard her purr that was the only regular noise in the room.

> Bernard Clavel

It is often said that the domestic cat is an exploiter of humans rather than the other way round. This is because he cat's solitary nature, demanding personality and secret night life set it apart from all other domestic animals.

> Juliet Clutton-Brock

I love cats because I enjoy my home; and little by little, they become its visible soul.

> Jean Cocteau

If I prefer cats to dogs, this is because there is no police cat.

> Jean Cocteau

Of all animals, cats, flies and women are those who lose least time washing.

> Jean Cocteau

The cat is the visible soul of the house.

> Jean Cocteau

All cats speak French.

> Sidonie Gabrielle Claudine Colette

At last! Someone who speaks French!

> Sidonie Gabrielle Claudine Colette

By associating with a cat, one only risks becoming richer.

> Sidonie Gabrielle Claudine Colette

Every cat, every tiger, embraces its prey and licks it just as is destroying it.

> Sidonie Gabrielle Claudine Colette

He dedicated quickly some ritual litanies which suited the characteristic graces and virtues of a cat called Chartreux, pure breed, small and perfect... My little bear with big cheeks... Fine... Fine... Pussy... My blue pigeon... pearl color demon...

> Sidonie Gabrielle Claudine Colette

I am indebted to the cat for a particular kind of honorable deceit, for a greater control over myself, for a characteristic aversion to brutal sounds, and for the need to keep silent for long periods of time.

> Sidonie Gabrielle Claudine Colette

It was a tabby, picked up in the fields where the misery of animals is great. Savage first, climbing up the walls if I closed her in, she had gained enough confidence and courage to become - at least she thought - the Queen of Cats.

> Sidonie Gabrielle Claudine Colette

Long and balanced on long legs, she walks with the uncertainty of virgins.

> Sidonie Gabrielle Claudine Colette

My cat does not talk as respectfully to me as I do to her.

> Sidonie Gabrielle Claudine Colette

Our perfect companions never have fewer than four feet.

> Sidonie Gabrielle Claudine Colette

Outside, the cat mewed to get in, and stood against the lowered fence scraping it like a harpist.

> Sidonie Gabrielle Claudine Colette

She was entrusted with kittens to lick, with puppies of foreign hounds.
Sidonie Gabrielle Claudine Colette

She was purring lustily, and in the darkness, she gave him a pussy kiss, putting her wet nose, for a moment, under the nose of Alain between the nostrils and the lip.
Sidonie Gabrielle Claudine Colette

The cat did not run away at my approach, but she hid as an eel does, at the precise second when I was to touch her.
Sidonie Gabrielle Claudine Colette

The cat pretends to forget and no longer gives him, in the garden, the favour of a look.
Sidonie Gabrielle Claudine Colette

The Siamese cat, previously at the height of comfort on the warm wall, suddenly opened her sapphire eyes in her mask of dark velvet...
Sidonie Gabrielle Claudine Colette

The sun played on her coat of Chartreux pussy, purple and blue like the breast of doves.
Sidonie Gabrielle Claudine Colette

There are no ordinary cats.
Sidonie Gabrielle Claudine Colette

Time spent with cats is never wasted.
Sidonie Gabrielle Claudine Colette

Tending a cat, the only risk is getting richer. Is it out of selfishness that for half a century I have been in search of his company?
Sidonie Gabrielle Claudine Colette

Why should I loudly crumple the condemned paper that the cat has been waiting for?
Sidonie Gabrielle Claudine Colette

Yes, in my life, there were lots of dogs but there was the Cat.
Sidonie Gabrielle Claudine Colette

You throw a ball to the cat, who miscalculates its momentum, on purpose, and lets it roll under the chair.
Sidonie Gabrielle Claudine Colette

While cats enjoyed their favourite virtual fantasies, mice were able to exploit the planet and live up to the full in the real world as in a big cheese.
Eoin Colfer

This cat may be the only witness to this horrible crime. I want this cat.
Colombo

It is easier to have relations with a poor cat than with a rich man.
Coluche

No tame animal has lost less of its native dignity or maintained more of its ancient reserve. The domestic cat might rebel tomorrow.
William Conway

A cat cares for you only as a source of food, security, and a place in the sun. Her high self-sufficiency is her charm.
Charles Horton Cooley

I do not like animals
They are full of fleas
And are smelly
However often you order
They do as they please.
François Coppée

Wikipedia is a fat cat that's showing off and boasting of its learning and knowledge
Yvon Corbeil

I never married because there was no need. I have three pets at home which answer the same purpose as a husband. I have a dog which growls every morning, a parrot which swears all afternoon, and a cat that comes home late at night.
Marie Corelli

Any conditioned cat-hater can be won over by any cat who chooses to make the effort.
Paul Corey

Father Christopher, in chains, breeches and boots, wandered into the village, peering at houses, stroking cats and teasing the women who did the laundry at the riverside.
Bernard Cornwell

It's a cat and you're his baby mouse.
Bernard Cornwell

The dog had promised never to bite
And the cat swore never to scratch
And since that day they have obeyed the order
And the dog and cat are friends forever.
Michèle Corti

Cats are designated friends.

Norman Corwin

I'm aloof, I like to run around outside, but I also like to curl up in warm spots. I eat fish.

Megan Coughlin

We need a word for all the kitty-prints all over my windshield because the cats like to lie on my hood when the car is still warm.

Megan Coughlin

What if it was cats who had invented technology? Would they have tv shows starring rubber squeak toys?

Douglas Coupland

I like the bed, it is the only place where, like the cat, I can sham death when breathing while being alive.

Arthur Cravan

White pussy, spotless pussy
I ask you, in these verses,
What secrets sleep in your green eyes,
What sarcasm under your whisker.

Charles Cros

If a cat does something, we call it instinct; if we do the same thing, for the same reason, we call it intelligence.

Will Cuppy

Cats come and go without ever leaving.

Martha Curtis

The cat has always been associated with the moon. Like the moon it comes to life at night, escaping from humanity and wandering over housetops with its eyes beaming out through the darkness.

Patricia Dale-Green

Chat, chat, chat, more chat, always cat.

Dalida & Delon

The grammarian ibn Babshad was sitting with his friends on the roof of a mosque in Cairo, eating some food. When a cat passed by, they gave her some morsels: she took them and ran away, only to come back time and time again. The scholars followed her and saw her running to an adjacent house on whose roof a blind cat was sitting. The cat carefully placed the morsels in front of her. Babshad was so moved by God's caring for the blind creature that he gave up all his belongings and lived in poverty, completely trusting in God until he died in 1067.

When sorrows press my heart, I say :
Maybe they'll disappear one day:
When books are my friends at night,
My darling then: the candle light,
My sweetest friend: a kitten white!

Damiri

I have an Egyptian cat. He leaves a pyramid in every room.

Rodney Dangerfield

I was so ugly when a baby that, when I was playing in the sandbox, the cat sent me some sand on my head to cover it.

Rodney Dangerfield

I call a spade a spade and a cat a pussy.

Frédéric Dard

To respect the cat is the beginning of the aesthetic sense.

Erasmus Darwin

A mathematician is a blind man in a dark room looking for a black cat which isn't there.

Charles Darwin

When a cat gives her confidence to a man this is his best gift.

Charles Darwin

Authors like cats because they are such quiet, lovable, wise creatures, and cats like authors for the same reasons.

Robertson Davies

Happiness is like a cat, if you try to cajole him, he escapes, if you do not mind him, he rubs against your legs and jumps on to your lap.

Robertson Davies

Perhaps God made cats so that man might have the pleasure of fondling the tiger...

Robertson Davies

The great charm of cats is their rampant egotism, their devil- may- care attitude toward responsibility, and their disinclination to earn an honest dollar.

Robertson Davies

The kitten has a luxurious, Bohemian, unpuritanical nature. It eats six meals a day, plays furiously with a toy mouse and a piece of rope, and suddenly falls into a deep sleep whenever the fit takes it. It never feels the necessity to do anything to justify its existence; it does not want to be a Good Citizen; it has never heard of Service. It knows that it is beautiful and delightful, and it considers that a sufficient contribution to the general good. And in return for its beauty and charm it expects fish, meat, and vegetables, a comfortable bed, a chair by the grate fire, and endless petting.

Robertson Davies

A simple push from a cat, a giant step for good taste.

Jim Davis (Garfield)

Ah, the great rivalry between cats and dogs!

Jim Davis (Garfield)

All kittens are cute until they grow up and become ugly.

Jim Davis (Garfield)

Among all species, cats are the most selfish.

Jim Davis (Garfield)

And cats will dominate the world!

Jim Davis (Garfield)

Caring for a cat is not easy but it's worth it.

Jim Davis (Garfield)

Cats also need Holidays.

Jim Davis (Garfield)

Cats are amazing creatures. Their manual has been missing for years.

Jim Davis (Garfield)

Cats are mysterious creatures.

Jim Davis (Garfield)

Cats are not known for their cooking.

Jim Davis (Garfield)

Cats are not only nice and cuddly.

Jim Davis (Garfield)

Cats can be very curious.

Jim Davis (Garfield)

Cats do not ask, they take.

Jim Davis (Garfield)

Cat hair! It's spring.

Jim Davis (Garfield)

Cats have extraordinary powers of perception.

Jim Davis (Garfield)

Cats have far too good manners to burp at the table.
Jim Davis (Garfield)

Cats have more success than ever.
Jim Davis (Garfield)

Cats have mystical powers.
Jim Davis (Garfield)

Cats have simple desires.
Jim Davis (Garfield)

Cats instinctively know dinner time.
Jim Davis (Garfield)

Cats love playing with empty boxes.
Jim Davis (Garfield)

Curiosity slaughters the cat.
Jim Davis (Garfield)

Cats too have feelings.
Jim Davis (Garfield)

Cats use claws to climb trees and the fire station to go down.
Jim Davis (Garfield)

Eating, sleeping, eating, sleeping, I, too, would like to be a cat.
Jim Davis (Garfield)

Even if I lived a hundred years, I would still not understand cats.
Jim Davis (Garfield)

Everyone on this planet loves cats. Whoever does not like them is an alien.
Jim Davis (Garfield)

For a cat, a sand castle is only a litter decorated with some towers.
Jim Davis (Garfield)

Formerly, cats were fearless, independent, strong and proud hunters.
Jim Davis (Garfield)

Having a cat reduces your blood pressure.
Jim Davis (Garfield)

How can anyone not love cats?
Jim Davis (Garfield)

How does one deal with an angry cat? With the greatest respect.
Jim Davis (Garfield)

I have been a dog for only two minutes and I already hate cats.

Jim Davis (Garfield)

I am only a cat but I feel that life is more complicated than people think.
Jim Davis (Garfield)

I do not know what I would have done without my cats.
Jim Davis (Garfield)

I found a purpose in life: scratch the cat's back.
Jim Davis (Garfield)

I never understood why cats like balls of wool.
Jim Davis (Garfield)

I suppose a house with a big cat must have a big mouse.
Jim Davis (Garfield)

I want to say to you, people, how much we cats appreciate you! If it were not you, who would feed us? Who would love us? And most important of all... Who would change our litter?
Jim Davis (Garfield)

I wonder what would happen to people without cats.
Wither and die, I think
I wonder what would happen to cats without people.
Who would change my litter?
Jim Davis (Garfield)

If a cat sneezes near a bride, it means she'll be happy all his life.
Jim Davis (Garfield)

If a cat sneezes the rain comes.
Jim Davis (Garfield)

If only cats could talk!
Jim Davis (Garfield)

If there is a patient in the family, wash the patient and throw the water on the cat.
Jim Davis (Garfield)

If you throw a ball to a dog, he will run and catch it. But this is not what a cat will do.
Jim Davis (Garfield)

It is amazing how long cats can just stare into space.
Jim Davis (Garfield)

It is comforting to have a warm cat on one's knees.
Jim Davis (Garfield)

It is not wise to bite the hand that feeds you.

It is so hot you could roast a cat on the sidewalk.
Jim Davis (Garfield)

It is true that cats always fall on their feet.
Jim Davis (Garfield)

It will take away your desire to have a cat for a while!
Jim Davis (Garfield)

Just when you think you know everything about your cat!
Jim Davis (Garfield)

Light cat food. Do I look like a light cat?
Jim Davis (Garfield)

Like all cats, I love exploring the unknown.
Jim Davis (Garfield)

Many cat owners reflect the grace, style and balance of their cat. Many cat owners are informed, sensitive, intelligent.
Jim Davis (Garfield)

Maybe Charlie Brown needs a cat?
Jim Davis (Garfield)

Never be condescending with a cat!
Jim Davis (Garfield)

New pants do not have cat hair.
Jim Davis (Garfield)

Nobody likes cold floors but we cats have to put twice two paws on them!
Jim Davis (Garfield)

Nothing is more difficult than waking a cat. Suddenly
Jim Davis (Garfield)

Once upon a time there was a cat who loved to eat...
Jim Davis (Garfield)

One life lost, eight still remain.
Jim Davis (Garfield)

One nice thing is to have another cat in the house.
Jim Davis (Garfield)

Owning a cat is a big responsibility.
Jim Davis (Garfield)

People who have pets live longer.
Jim Davis (Garfield)

Pets have their fifteen minutes of madness.
Jim Davis (Garfield)

Simple cat, simple pleasures.
Jim Davis (Garfield)

The cat is constantly in motion. I do not personally know this cat, but I've heard of it.
Jim Davis (Garfield)

The cat is the best hunter in the world.
Jim Davis (Garfield)

The cat is the center of the universe.
Jim Davis (Garfield)

The difference between relaxation and exercise for the cat is too subtle to be understood by ordinary mortals.
Jim Davis (Garfield)

The human brain is much bigger than the cat's. Big and bulky.
Jim Davis (Garfield)

There is always somebody to rescue cats.
Jim Davis (Garfield)

There are countries where people eat cats.
Jim Davis (Garfield)

There is more than one way to skin a cat.
Jim Davis (Garfield)

There is nothing that can stop a cat having a nap.
Jim Davis (Garfield)

Way down deep, we're all motivated by the same urges. Cats have the courage to live by them.
Jim Davis (Garfield)

We cats are unique.
Jim Davis (Garfield)

We cats are very possessive.
Jim Davis (Garfield)

We cats have a sixth sense for these things.
Jim Davis (Garfield)

We cats can talk but we prefer to keep silent.
Jim Davis (Garfield)

We are very mysterious: eating, sleeping, eating, sleeping...

We cats have not invented the nap. But we raised it to perfection.
Jim Davis (Garfield)

Welcome to a bright day with your favourite cat.
Jim Davis (Garfield)

What a horrible nightmare, I dreamed I was a dog!
Jim Davis (Garfield)

What do we get if we remove half the brain of a cat? An intelligent dog! Author's note: do not compare the dog and the cat to man and woman...
Jim Davis (Garfield)

What would life be like if it was cats and dogs who were in charge?
Jim Davis (Garfield)

What is special about the friendship between animals and their masters? May each of us need to be loved?
Jim Davis (Garfield)

When a cat gives you a dead, fragrant thing, it is a form of love.
Jim Davis (Garfield)

Why did God create me? To feed the cat.
Jim Davis (Garfield)

Why give a name to a pet who does not mind you when you call?
Jim Davis (Garfield)

Woe to him who attracts the wrath of a cat.
Jim Davis (Garfield)

You are always in my legs, thank you.
Jim Davis (Garfield)

You are the cat, I am the master!
Jim Davis (Garfield)

You have decided to have animals who love you, so you're not a failure.
Jim Davis (Garfield)

You know, cats are supposed to eat mice.
Jim Davis (Garfield)

You must know what motivates a cat.
Jim Davis (Garfield)

You never know what cats think.
Jim Davis (Garfield)

You noticed how cats know how to blend into the environment?

Jim Davis (Garfield)

A common cat is worth four legal pence...
Hywel Dda

One pound is the worth of one of the king's pet animals.
Hywel Dda

A cat attracted by the noise came mewing, threaded his way through the legs of his master and then left.
Jean-Louis Debré

I'll draw a Republican cat for you. You do not know? Well, the first eye is blue, the nose is white and the second eye is red.
Jean-Louis Debré

I made friends with a charming Angora cat who followed me and let me caress him.
Eugène Delacroix

Animals attack animals to eat. Not for fun!
Alain Delon

To me, one who causes suffering to animals is worse than a beast. He is an animal himself.
Alain Delon

The day when we're gone, there will remain animals. They will be quieter than with us around.
Alain Delon

A cat with kittens nearly always decides sooner or later to move them.
Sidney Denham

Although all cat games have their rules and rituals, these vary with the individual player. The cat, of course, never breaks a rule. If it does not follow precedent, that simply means it has created a new rule and it is up to you to learn it quickly if you want the game to continue.
Sidney Denham

When choosing a pet, remember that a dog will consider you as his family, and a cat as a domestic.
Ron Dentinger

Prince, often we deliberate,
But we can say, like the rat
About advice that fails:
Who will hang the bell to the cat's tail?
Eustache Deschamps

There must be some similarities between the people who dislike cats. Something a little curt in their movements. In their bodies. A certain lack of sensuality.
Régine Desforges

I never noticed that there was so much difference between dogs and cats!
Desperate Housewives

It's stupid, a cat!
Desperate Housewives

How strange, the cat is no more on grandmother, she is probably cold.
Pierre Desproges

After being neutered, most often by his mistress, the cat will be cherished by her for the rest of his days.
Louis-Ferdinand Destouches (Céline)

For my part, tell yourself have other fish to fry than rushing at the tanks and hurling myself under them!...
Louis-Ferdinand Destouches (Céline)

A cat... would check to see if you brought anything to eat, and if not, would turn and walk away, his tail held high.
Mike Deupree

When a cat chooses to be friendly, it's a big deal, because a cat is picky.
Mike Deupree

If he is comical, it is only because of the incongruity of so demure a look and so wild a heart.
Alan Devoe

Cats look beyond appearances - beyond species entirely, it seems - to peer into the heart.
Barbara L. Diamond

Cats may, indeed, be the thinking man's pet - because living with cats certainly keeps you on your toes!
Barbara L. Diamond

Chances are that a man who can nuzzle a kitten is also open and caring in other facets of his life.
Barbara L. Diamond

Don't let anyone tell you that loving a cat is silly. Love, in any form, is a precious commodity.
Barbara L. Diamond

Does the father figure in your cat's life ever clean the litter box? My husband claims that men lack the scooping gene.
Barbara L. Diamond

How nice it is to think that feline dreams, like our own, are painted with creative brush strokes from time to time. Perhaps my cats and I even share the same dream: a world where all kittens are wanted and loved, and where every cat has a safe, warm place to sleep in... and to dream.
Barbara L. Diamond

It isn't always easy being a father to a cat.
Barbara L. Diamond

The purr from cat to man says, 'You bring me happiness; I am at peace with you.'
Barbara L. Diamond

The whir of a can opener or the bark of an unfamiliar dog... will send even the most deeply dozing cat bounding into the kitchen or under the bed.
Barbara L. Diamond

Your cat may never have to hunt farther than the kitchen counter for its supper or face a predator fiercer than the vacuum cleaner...
Barbara L. Diamond

He opened the door and this time most cats managed to sneak into the hut.
Philip K. Dick

The cats, joined by a small dog, came up and walked under his feet, preventing it from moving as he tried to leave the hut.
Philip K. Dick

The cat jumped down from the shelves at man level; three old orange tomcats and a silky cat of the Isle of Man, then several half-Siamese kittens, with tapered and mustached muzzles, a young black cat, and finally with great difficulty, a female cat expecting babies.
Philip K. Dick

What greater gift than the love of a cat?
Charles Dickens

You remember my ideal cat always has a huge rat in its mouth, just going out of sight - though going out of sight holds a peculiar pleasure of its own.
Emily Dickinson

There are cats and cats.
Denis Diderot

Everybody wants to be a Cat.
Walt Disney

If somebody sees that there are mice here, I risk losing my job.
Walt Disney

If you want to keep your marrowbones, you'd better learn to love cats.
Walt Disney

Spices, it picks old cats up.
Walt Disney

When a baby moves in, the dog moves out.
Walt Disney

Some people say that cats are sneaky, evil, and cruel. True, and they have many other fine qualities as well.
Missy Dizick

Actually, cats do this to protect you from gnomes who come and steal your breath while you sleep.
John Dobbin

There are people who reshape the world by force or argument, but the cat just lies there, dozing, and the world quietly reshapes itself to suit his comfort and convenience.
Allen and Ivy Dodd

I was the wild cat.
Arielle Dombasle

Some people are uncomfortable with the idea that humans belong to the same class of animals as cats and cows and raccoons. They're like the people who become successful and then don't want to be reminded of the old neighborhood.
Phil Donahue

Cats seem to have an innate understanding of the pleasures of life that humans often forget. We can learn a lot by closely observing our feline friends.
Glenn Dromgoole

If a man sees himself in a dream looking at a large cat, it is a good omen and means that a large harvest will come to him.
The Dream Book

I shudder to admit it, but I hate the sound of the violin, these high-pitched sounds scratch my ears. I'm like these people that wince as they touch a cat.
François-René Duchâble

His agitation was so great she placed the cat food under the dog's nose and the dog soup under the cat's nose.
Alexandre Dumas

One day on opening the shutters of your house, intrigued by cries you hear deep in your garden, you go out to find the origin of them and there under the pile of wood, you are face to face with a small frightened hairball : a kitten.
Pierre-Yves Dumoulin

One of the quickest routes to a cat's brain is through its stomach.
Ian Dunbar

I have a reasonable love for cats.
Annie Duperey

People who love cats are often chilly.
Annie Duperey

People who love cats are skillful enough to flee conflicts and defend themselves when they are badly assaulted.
Annie Duperey

People who love cats sometimes do have excessive confidence in intuition.
Annie Duperey

People who love cats avoid power struggles.
Annie Duperey

People who love cats love their independence because this is what ensures their freedom.
Annie Duperey

People who love cats would like to be loved with respect and tenderness.
Annie Duperey

The silence of cats is contagious.
Annie Duperey

What is wonderful with a cat, is that when it comes up to you, there is nothing to do except to watch it.
Annie Duperey

Many cats simply pounce only on their own drummers.
Karen Duprey

Most cats are not shy about letting their masters know what they want.
Karen Duprey

Like a cat stretching out, the shadow of the house extends into the yard, scratching the steps at the gate. This is the time when the garden is waiting for our arrival.
Chantal Dupuy-Dunier

To all cats who left for "I don't know what heaven"
Hoping to see them again one day.
Joëlle Dutillet

At ten, she was as thin as a cat, at seventeen, she had not, as they say, tumbled.
Jean Dutourd

No amount of time can erase the memory of a good cat, and no amount of masking tape can ever totally remove his fur from your couch.
Leo Dworken

If a homeless cat could talk, it would probably say, 'Give me shelter, food, companionship and love, and I will be yours for life!
Susan Easterly

People who love cats have some of the biggest hearts around.
Susan Easterly

The key to a successful new relationship between a cat and a human is patience.
Susan Easterly

In the beginning, God created man, but seeing him so feeble, He gave him the cat.
Warren Eckstein

To the pure geometer the radius of curvature is an incidental characteristic - like the grin of the Cheshire cat. To the physicist it is an indispensable characteristic. It would be going too far to say that to the physicist the cat is merely incidental to the grin. Physics is concerned with interrelatedness such as the interrelatedness of cats and grins. In this case the cat without a grin and the grin without a cat are equally set aside as purely mathematical fantasies.
Sir Arthur Stanley Eddington

Curiosity is the very basis of education and if you tell me that curiosity killed the cat, I'll only say the cat died nobly.
Arnold Edinborough

People that don't like cats haven't met the right one yet.
Deborah A. Edwards

To my mind here is nothing in the animal world, more delightful than grown cats at play. They are so swift and light and graceful, so subtle and designing, and yet so richly comical.
Monica Edwards

A man must work hard for people to remember him. A cat does it easily. He has only to appear and his presence remains for years on rainy days.
Albert Einstein

You see, the wire telegraph is a kind of a very, very long cat. You pull his tail in New York and his head is mewing in Los Angeles. Do you understand this? And the radio operates exactly the same way: you send signals here, they receive them there. The only difference is that there is no cat.
Albert Einstein

Cats don't bark – and consumers today don't salivate on command as they seemed to do a couple of decades ago. Consumers today behave more like cats than Pavlov's pooch. Times have changed – and so have we probably.
Bryan Eisenberg

Animals are such agreeable friends - they ask no questions, they pass no criticism.
George Eliot

I'm not one o' those as can see the cat i' the dairy, an' wonder what she's come after.
George Eliot

When you see a cat in deep meditation, the reason, I tell you, is always the same: his mind is lost in bottomless contemplation. At the thought of the thought of the thought of his name: Mysterious and inaccessible Singular Name.
Thomas Stearns Eliott

Again I must remind you that a dog's a dog - a cat's a cat.
Thomas Stearns Eliott

Macavity, Macavity, there's no one like Macavity, there never was a cat of such deceitfulness and suavity.
Thomas Stearns Eliott

When a cat adopts you there is nothing else to do than stand and wait until the wind turns.
Thomas Stearns Eliott

The naming of cats is a difficult matter. It isn't just one of your holiday games. You may think at first I'm mad as a hatter. When I tell you a cat must have three different names...
Thomas Stearns Eliott

A cat needs a specific name, a specific and solemn enough name, otherwise how could he lift the tail straight, or develop his whiskers, or maintain his pride?
Thomas Stearns Eliott

You have learned enough to see that cats are much like you and me.
Thomas Stearns Eliott

Cats standing on the ledge drooled at the idea of eating fish. They were kicking legs and chattering jaws, never catching their prey. The koi had sonar and radar.
James Ellroy

He collected the stray cats. It did not take account of their faults. He sought distraction.
James Ellroy

He then equipped the suite to withstand the cat. The cat loved the result. The cat perched. The cat jumped. The cat killed the mice coming out of the walls.
James Ellroy

Do say something! You look like the cat that ate the canary.
James Ellroy

The cat cornered a rat. A bite. Goodbye.
He picked up the rat. The cat showed his teeth.
James Ellroy

The cat spat. The cat showed its teeth. The cat was pacing his cage.
James Ellroy

They took the cat. They took a suite. The cat vandalized.
He tore the curtains. He shitted on chairs. He killed the birds on the terrace. He plundered the dishes brought by the room servers.
James Ellroy

Cats, for example, I don't like.

Gad Elmaleh

The cat is too big a beast.
Histail reaches his head
He turns in a circle
And responds to caresses.

Paul Éluard

Do you see that kitten chasing her own tail so prettily? If you could look with her eyes, you might see her surrounded with hundreds of figures performing complex dramas, with tragic and comic issues, long conversations, many characters, many ups and downs of fate.
Ralph Waldo Emerson

A cat is the only domestic animal I know who washes its hind-quarters and does a damned impressive job of it.
Joseph Epstein

Goldfish: a pet which, compared to the cat, has the advantage that he tears less at the curtains of the living room.
Marc Escayrol

Tabby Cat: The only breed cat you can buy in supermarkets because their integrated bar code facilitates the checkout.
Marc Escayrol

A cat, having fallen in love with a handsome young man, begged Aphrodite to transform her into a woman.
Esope

O cat of lapis lazuli, great of forms… mistress of the embalming house, grant peace to the beautiful West.
Papyrus d'Espaheran

You say that Philippe Bouvard roams the neighborhood on the edge of pets' bowls and extorts money from the cat and terrorizes it?!!
Eulalie

I was only a small child when the seeds of cat enchantment were sown within me.
May Eustace

Some cats are blind and stone deaf but ain't no cat wuz ever dumb.
Anthony Henderson Euwer

When your dog jumps on to your bed that is because he loves your company. When your cat jumps on to your bed, that is because he loves your bed.
Alisha Everett

The look of the place was reminiscent of a good-natured woman and this was confirmed by the presence on the walls of engravings showing a basket of kittens, deer in the woods and returning haymakers.
René Fallet

We have a theory that cats are planning to take over the world, just try to look them straight in the eye... yup, they're hiding something!
Dog Fancy

My sorrows will be over when I find companionship in a cat.
Ahmad ibn Faris

It always gives me a shiver when I see a cat seeing what I can't see.
Eleanor Farjeon

While sipping slowly like a cat, she dipped her eyes in those of the Perigordian.
Frank Ferrand

Melancholy is a lost cat believed to have been found again.
Léo Ferré

A sturdy lad… who teams it, farms it… and always like a cat falls on his feet, is worth a hundred of these city dolls.
Marsilio Ficino

In the last century, a priest who lived in the company of a large cat, suddenly showed all the signs of certain death.
Elian J. Finbert

In women's prisons in England, women are allowed to bring in their cat so that it shares their time of imprisonment with them.
Elian J. Finbert

The cat was nursing puppies and her own kittens, and the bitch, conversely, did the same. So that we could see the kittens follow the bitch and puppies, the cat.
Elian J. Finbert

For us the cat is the hot, hairy, mustachioed and purring memory of a lost paradise.
Léonor Fini

Almost everybody can be imagined as either a cat or a dog.
F. Scott Fitzgerald

Unless, he added turning to his wife, you'd like to be alone, my little cat?
Gustave Flaubert

When God made the world, He chose to put animals in it, and decided to give each whatever it wanted. All the animals formed a long line before His throne, and the cat quietly went to the end of the line. To the elephant and the bear He gave strength, to the rabbit and the deer, swiftness; to the owl, the ability to see at night, to the birds and the butterflies, great beauty; to the fox, cunning; to the monkey, intelligence; to the dog, loyalty; to the lion, courage; to the otter, playfulness. And all these were things the animals begged of God. At last he came to the end of the line, and there sat the little cat, waiting patiently. What will YOU have? God asked the cat.

The cat shrugged modestly. Oh, whatever scraps you have left over. I don't mind.

But I'm God. I have everything left over.

Then I'll have a little of everything, please.

And God gave a great shout of laughter at the cleverness of this small animal, and gave the cat everything she asked for, adding grace and elegance and, only for her, a gentle purr that would always attract humans and assure her a warm and comfortable home.

But he took away her false modesty.

Lenore Fleischer

When you're special to a cat, you're special indeed... she brings to you the gift of her preference of you, the sight of you, the sound of your voice, the touch of your hand.

Leonore Fleisher

If their claws didn't retract, cats would be like Velcro.

Dr. Bruce Fogle

Ellen grew up in an almost entirely male house. She cut her hair, wore a dagger and learned not to play with kittens or worry about the old blind dogs.

Ken Follett

It reminded him of the picture of a cat, smooth and sensual, with its glossy skin.

Ken Follett

There was no hunting that day, so young people of the castle were playing at one of their favourite games: the cat stone. The castle was home to still a large number of cats, one more or one less will not change anything.
They closed the doors and shutters of the room in the dungeon, then pushed the furniture against the wall so the cat had no hiding place and then they put a pile of stones in the middle of the room. The cat, an old gray cat, felt in the air the thirst for blood and sat near the door, waiting for a chance to slip away.

Each player would put a penny in the pot for each stone he threw and it was he who threw the fatal stone that gained the pot.
Ken Follett

They had tied a cat to a stake, leaving only the head and legs free. The fun was to kill him while having one's hands tied behind one's back. The only way to do this was to knock the unfortunate animal's head. The cat, of course, defended himself, claws out, and bit his attacker's face.
Ken Follett

When I was young, I confused leper and leopard and I imagined the lepers' island inhabited by spotted lions.
Ken Follett

When no meeting was held, the owner threw a cat in the duck pond and set four dogs on him, a game that caused great laughter among drinkers.
Ken Follett

In the life we lead today, I think the cat is the last representative of Paradise on Earth. This is both the most domestic and wildest animal at the same time.
Rémo Forlani

Until one has loved an animal, part of their soul remains unawakened.
Anatole France

A cat can sleep anywhere, anytime.
Jacqueline Francis

Bin, it's Cheese, my gray mouse. I want Cheese and the cat to get used to living in peace. But I am prudent: for a start, I've made a little armor.
Frankin (Gaston Lagaffe)

Here's the cat. Since he first tasted my cooking, he will not leave me.
Frankin (Gaston Lagaffe)

I do not know if the cat would attack the gull... But he could catch the mouse... the mouse, she would not hurt the goldfish, but I wonder if a seagull is capable of eating a mouse... or a goldfish... And cats love fish!... And open your eye: I'm always afraid that the mouse could fall into the water of the goldfish.
Frankin (Gaston Lagaffe)

Shhh! You'll have to do without me. The cat is asleep so I have not the heart to wake him up.
Frankin (Gaston Lagaffe)

S'so! You do not know that a cat can't stand closed doors!? And that he needs to feel free?

Frankin (Gaston Lagaffe)

A countryman between two lawyers is like a fish between two cats.
Benjamin Franklin

The cat in gloves catches no mice.
Benjamin Franklin

Four little Persians, but only one looked in my direction. I extended a tentative finger and two soft paws clung to it. There was a contented sound of purring, I suspect, on both parts.
George Freedley

Cats, women and serious criminals have in common that they represent an unattainable ideal and an ability to love themselves that makes them attractive to us.
Sigmund Freud

I rarely meddled in the cat's personal affairs and she rarely meddled in mine. Neither of us was foolish enough to attribute human emotions to our pets.
Kinky Friedman

The smart cat doesn't let anyone know who he is.
H.G. Frommer

Cats exist in our world to disprove the dogma that all things were created to serve man.
Froquevielle

Nothing's more playful than a young cat, nor graver than an old one.
Thomas Fuller

His Majesty the cat does not wallow in the mud. Lies and manipulations are beyond his reach...
Audray Gaillard

This is the story of Wouaf wouaf-Sarko, Aquarius dog, and Mew de Villepin, Scorpion cat...
Audray Gaillard

Men are like dogs, they come when called. Women are like cats, just call them and they will disperse.
Michel Galabru

Clinging to this thing like fleas on a cat.
Battlestar Galactica

The cat dropped the rat between its two front paws. There are those, it said with a sigh, in tones as smooth as oiled silk, who have suggested that the tendency of a cat to play with its prey is a merciful one - after all, it permits the occasional funny running little snack to escape, from time to time. How often does your dinner manage to escape?

Neil Gaiman

Everything a cat is and does physically is to me beautiful, lovely, stimulating, soothing, attractive and an enchantment.

Paul Gallico

There is the little matter of disposing of one's droppings in which the cat is far ahead of its rivals. The dog is somehow thrilled by what he or any of his friends have produced, hates to leave it, adores smelling it, and sometimes eats it... The cat covers it up if he can...

Paul Gallico

Twenty-seven cats at one time hints at monomania, but in my case it was simpler. If you like cats and have some, you get kittens; and if you like kittens and enjoy having them about, they grow up and beget more cats for you.

Paul Gallico

We recognize the true greatness of a nation from its treatment of animals.

Mohandas Mahatma Gandhi

The mice which find themselves helplessly caught between a cat's teeth acquire no merit from their enforced sacrifice.

Mohandas Mahatma Gandhi

Never seeming to give oneself entirely, being able to snatch oneself away so that no link, no matter how strong, exempts one from being oneself, that's why cats so often change common tastes.

Gilbert Ganne

Cats are the only living beings who know they are equal to men.

Julie Gardiner

Don't think that I'm silly for liking it, I just happen to like the simple little things, and I love cats!

Michelle Gardner

Men have shaped dogs to their will. Cats are exactly the same as they were about ten million years.

Marion Garretty

Poets generally love cats – because poets have no delusions about their own superiority.

Marion Garretty

Very few people are lucky enough to have a wild animal as a friend. Cats excepted, of course.
Marion Garretty

Her function is to sit and be admired.
Georgina Strickland Gates

A black coat,
Wild and beautiful it was, that of a she-cat
Whose deep blue eyes sparkling in the night
Fascinated me with their reflections of agate.
Emmanuel-Henri Gaudicour

A Cat, with its phosphorescent eyes that shine like lanterns and sparks flashing from its back, moves fearlessly through the darkness, where it meets wandering ghosts, witches, alchemists, necromancers, grave-robbers, lovers, thieves, murderers, grey-cloaked patrols, and all the obscene larvae that only emerge at night.
Théophile Gautier

Cats thrive in silence, order and tranquility.
Théophile Gautier

I love cats. Cats are the tigers of us poor devils.
Théophile Gautier

Herod, Blazius and Scapin, who were on their mouths and hungry as sanctimonious cats, licking their chops at this eloquence so fat, so delicious.
Théophile Gautier

If you are worthy of its affection, a cat will be your friend, but never your slave.
Théophile Gautier

The cat is a dilettante in fur.
Théophile Gautier

The cat's eyes, fixed on the bird with fascinating intensity, said in a speech that the parrot could hear very well and had nothing ambiguous about it: "While green, this chicken should be good to eat."
Théophile Gautier

Man complains that he lives! Does he not have hands to stroke the fur of cats!
Théophile Gautier

Sometimes he sits in front of you with eyes so melting, so caressing, and so human that they almost frighten you, because it is impossible to believe that there is not a soul there.
Théophile Gautier

Who can believe that there is no soul behind those luminous eyes!
Théophile Gautier

If cats were friendlier to mice, mice would no longer be afraid of cats. And it would be really easy to catch them.
Philippe Geluck (Le Chat)

Around each kitten there seemed to be floating pollen dust, a small blonde light that did not fade in the sunlight.
Maurice Genevoix

A cat is a hand-fed tiger.
Vakaoka Genrin

Cats know how to obtain food without labour, shelter without confinement, and love without penalties.
Walter Lionel George

According to Zysla Bellia, cats prefer Ruquier and Delarue to Drucker. Normal, within Drucker, there is his dog, Olga
Valérie Ghezail

In a fire, between a Rembrandt and a cat, I would save the cat.
Alberto Giacometti

From yard to yard there was seen wandering a number of starving cats.
André Gide

He plays with us like a cat with a mouse he torments...
André Gide

I would like the pope to live in a small villa with two cats.
Père Guy Gilbert

The gray cat that he had disturbed in the living room, last night, put his head through the cat flap..., slid through, extricating his feet from the hole, one after another, came up and rubbed against him while purring.
Jean Giono

We do not own a cat, he it is who owns us.
Françoise Giroud

One day, we discovered a little soft thing, fragile and worn, hard of hearing, with uncertain walk, short of breath, memory declining, talking

with a cat in solitude on a Sunday. It's called aging, and it's pure scandal to me.
Françoise Giroud

Ouch! A tigress... an enormous tigress full of feet who confused my arse with a football!
Godi + Zidrou (l'élève Ducobu)

As soon as you start to caress a cat's back, you have no right to stop anymore!
Witold Gombrowicz

Here is an old cat who does not play, doesn't arch his back anymore and runs away whenever he sees a child: this is experience.
Edmond and Jules de Goncourt

This cat's glance, deep, mysteriously investigating, almost disturbing in its fixity, this eye open on you like a machine taking your picture, makes one think that cats are better judges of people who approach them than dogs are.
Edmond and Jules de Goncourt

We slandered cats. They have tenderness and intelligent affection. When I feel well, the cat jumps onto the foot of my bed and is quite quiet and when I feel sick, she sleeps against my chest, as she hates my beard, she licks my nose from time to time as if to give me a kiss.
Edmond and Jules de Goncourt

We speak to a woman, we say sentences that we know she does not understand, as when we talk to a dog or a cat.
Edmond and Jules de Goncourt

When kittens are born in a laundry basket, it does not automatically make socks of them.
Terry Goodkind

When once you've been scratched by a cat, you will remember it for the rest of your days.
Terry Goodkind

Cats are the ultimate narcissists. You can tell this by all the time they spend on personal grooming. Dogs aren't like this. A dog's idea of personal grooming is to roll himself over a dead fish.
James Gorman

I have a frog in my throat. Had it been a cat, he would have had no milk.
Jean-Marie Gourio

The citizen is a variety of man, a degenerate or primitive variety, he is to man what the alley cat is to a wildcat.
                                                Rémy de Gourmont

He has become a much better cat than I a person. Hs gentle urgings made me realize that life doesn't end just because one has a few obstacles to overcome.
                                                Mary F. Graf

Do not meddle in the affairs of cats, for they are subtle and will piss on your computer.
                                                Bruce Graham

Prose books are the show dogs I breed and sell to support my cat.
                                                Robert Graves

After scolding one's cat one looks into its face and is seized by the ugly suspicion that it understood every word. And has filed it for reference.
                                                Charlotte Gray

Any cat who misses a mouse pretends it was aiming at the dead leaf.
                                                Charlotte Gray

Two people meeting for the first time suddenly relax if they find they both have cats. And plunge into anecdote.
                                                Charlotte Gray

All cats like being the focus of attention.
                                                Peter Gray

Cats are kind masters, just as long as you remember your station.
                                                Paul Gray

Cats were put into the world to disprove the dogma that all things were created to serve man.
                                                Paul Gray

One must love a cat on its own terms.
                                                Paul Gray

What female heart can despise gold? What cat's averse to fish?
                                                Thomas Gray

There is, incidentally, no way of talking about cats that enables one to come off as a sane person.
                                                Dan Greenberg

Cats are dangerous companions for writers because cat watching is a near-perfect method of failing to write anything.
                                                Dan Greenberg

If your cat favours its left paw, chances are that it possesses psychic ability to some extent.
Dr. David Greene

In performing a variety of intellectually demanding tasks, cats usually emerge as clear winners (over dogs).
Dr. David Greene

Cats are not redundant, they are precious gifts from God.
Grégoire Ist

I have yet to be a godfather: the child is completely black with only white tips on his paws and not a single white hair on the body, which happens only once every two years.
Grimm brothers

Fans think they want to see more than the 10 to 20 seconds of Itchy and Scratchy that we put in on the show, but my feeling is that less is more. Once you've skinned and flayed a cat, ripped his head off, made him drink acid and tied his tongue to the moon, there really isn't that much to say.
Matt Groening

He was lost! not a shade of doubt as to that;
For he never barked at a slinking cat.
Arthur Guiterman

THE DOG'S COLD NOSE

When Noah, perceiving 'twas time to embark
Persuaded the creatures to enter the Ark
The dog, with a friendliness truly sublime
Assisted in herding them.
Two at a time He drove in the elephants, zebras and gnus
Until they were packed like a boxful of screws,
The cat in the cupboard, the mouse on the shelf,
The bug in the crack; then he backed in himself.
But such was the lack of available space
He couldn't tuck all of him into the place;
So after the waters had flooded the plain
And down from the heavens fell blankets of rain
He stood with his muzzle thrust out through the door
The whole forty days of that terrible pour!
Because of which drenching, zoologists hold,
The nose of a healthy dog always is cold!
Arthur Guiterman

Cat lovers can readily be identified. Their clothes always look old and worn. Their sheets look like bath towels and their bath looks like a collection of knitting mistakes.
Eric Gurney

The really great thing about cats is their endless variety. One can pick a cat that will fit almost any kind of decor, color, scheme, income, personality, mood. But under the fur, whatever color it may be, there still lies, essentially unchanged, one of the world's free souls.
Eric Gurney

Cats are concealed, they say. My cat was secret, but she tasted as much pleasure in showing his secret as hiding it.
Paul Guth

In the kingdom of cats, the camel is not a mail cat.
Didier Hallépée

Cuddly cat, happy master
Distant cat, grief master.
Didier Hallépée

A Half-god himself, he attracted Pharaoh. No doubt he knows how to seduce you now.
Didier Hallépée

Only the lioness can throw herself unscathed into the mouth of the lion. Or practically so.
Didier Hallépée

Should we prefer our mau cat to our wife? Your cat loves you with unconditional love, Your wife must be reconquered every day. If your wife runs away, you'll be too unhappy to give your mau cat all the love he deserves.
Didier Hallépée

Sleeping is a little bit like dying.
No matter since I have nine lives!
Didier Hallépée

Deep through his enigmatic gaze, 40 centuries of feline friendship look down on you.
Didier Hallépée

It takes about 63 days for a cat to give birth to a litter of five kittens. The fact that you only want one kitten will not shrink that period to 12 days!
Didier Hallépée

Deep down, the cat is cat. That's what makes him so beautiful.

Didier Hallépée

Cats are like husbands: when you allow them to wander, you are not sure to see them back!

Didier Hallépée

Once you have taste the pleasures of maus, you cannot do without them.
All the rest is literature.

Didier Hallépée

You may have a cat in the room with you with no anxiety about anything except eatables. The presence of a cat is positively soothing to a student.

Philip Gilbert Hamerton

Which is more beautiful - feline movement or feline stillness?

Elizabeth Hamilton

What's virtue in a man can't be virtue in a cat.

Gail Hamilton

Cats are much like what they used to be when they were first domesticated. They are very independent because they had to be in order to survive.

Dr. Raymond Hampton

You never saw such a crazy cat. 'Up the wall' took on a literal meaning with him.

Arnold Hano

Who hath a better friend than a cat?

William Hardwin

In my days, we didn't have dogs or cats. All I had was Silver Beauty, my beloved paper clip.

Jennifer Hart

Cats are mysterious and marvelous companions.

Frédérique Hébrard

In the beginning was the cat...

Frédérique Hébrard

He is not only a witness to the lives of his masters (masters?), he is a key actor. He knows things that we do not know, he teaches us.

Frédérique Hébrard

These are sacred, inaccessible beings. Gods.

Frédérique Hébrard

Anyone who considers protocol unimportant has never dealt with a cat.

Robert A. Heinlein

While the rest of the human race evolved from apes, redheads evolved from cats.

Robert A. Heinlein

Cats, like butterflies, need no excuse.

Robert A. Heinlein

How we behave toward cats here below determines our status in heaven.

Robert A. Heinlein

Theology is never any help; it is searching in a dark cellar at midnight for a black cat that isn't there. Theologians can persuade themselves of anything.

Robert A. Heinlein

There is no such thing as 'just a cat'.

Robert A. Heinlein

Women and cats will do as they please, and men and dogs should relax and get used to the idea.

Robert A. Heinlein

The most ignorant and most confident said that a cat would suck the breath out of a baby and kill him.

Ernest Hemingway

A cat has absolute emotional honesty: human beings, for one reason or another, may hide their feelings, but a cat does not.

Ernest Hemingway

One cat just leads to another.

Ernest Hemingway

The cat's origins are lost in the mists of time... in legends and folklore... in religious myths and parables.

Fiona and Marc Henrie

As there are dog and cat in each sex, we have to be alternately dogs with cats and cats with dogs.

Marie-Jean Hérault de Séchelles

A cat is a pygmy lion who loves mice, hates dogs, and patronizes human beings.

Oliver Herford

You can't save a cat by stopping time.

Heroes

Cats are connoisseurs of comfort.

A cat doesn't know what it wants and wants more of it.
James Herriot

Richard Hexem

A woman hath nine lives like a cat.
Georges Heywood

It needs had to be a wily mouse that should breed in the cat's ear.
John Heywood

The cat would eat fish, and would not wet her paws.
John Heywood

When all candles be out, all cats be gray.
John Heywood

A cat is a living work of art.
Patricia Highsmith

A cat makes a house into a home.
Patricia Highsmith

A writer is never lonely with a cat.
Patricia Highsmith

Cats offer writers something that humans cannot provide: a company that is neither protest nor disturbance and that is as soothing and changing as a very calm sea.
Patricia Highsmith

When you are going to die, all the animals that you knew will come and form a chain to hoist you into heaven.
Hindu legend

If your cat falls from a tree, go indoors and have a good laugh.
Patricia Hitchcock

There are few things in life more heartwarming than to be welcomed by a cat.
Tay Hohoff

A catless writer is almost inconceivable. It's a perverse taste, really, since it would be easier to write even with a herd of buffaloes in the room than with one cat; cats make their nest among the notes and bite the end of the pen and walk on the typewriter keys.
Barbara Holland

There is no cat 'language'. Painful as it is for us to admit, they don't need one.
Barbara Holland

Essentially, you do not so much teach your cat as bribe him.
Lynn Hollyn

Just as the would-be debutante will fret and fuss over every detail till all is perfect, so will the fastidious feline patiently toil until every whisker tip is in place.
Lynn Hollyn

I have noticed that what cats appreciate most in a human being is not his or her ability to produce food, which they take for granted--but his or her entertainment value.
Geoffrey Household

It doesn't do to be sentimental about cats; the best ones won't respect you for it.
Susan Howatch

The way to keep a cat is to try to chase it away.
E. W. Howe

Adopt a cat is above all adopt his feline nature with its many paradoxes: alternation of docility and insubordination, a mixture of sweetness and apparent cruelty, a good mix of dedication and feigned selflessness.
Marie-Luce Hubert

If the dog embodies action, the cat is rather a symbol of reflection.
Marie-Luce Hubert

Cats at firesides live luxuriously and are the picture of comfort.
Leigh Hunt

From sucking cat to suffering cat, the same note remains. Purring, the cat gives herself body and soul.
Jean-Louis Hue

.The first time the cat purrs is when he sucks
Jean-Louis Hue

A house without a cat is an aquarium without fish.
Jean-Louis Hue

God made the cat so that man might have the pleasure of caressing the tiger.
Victor Hugo

We equip the cat with old rags,
And then we put him to bed with the doll.
Nini scolds the cat when his dress is wrinkled,
And the other day, the cat bit me to the bone.
Victor Hugo

By living with his pet, the child will gain many human qualities that he will keep as an adult. The animal allows him to develop his personality, his sense of responsibility, responds to his emotional needs and his desire to communicate. In him he also finds comfort in any conflict with his parents or his friends at school. His four-legged friend accepts him for what he is and does not judge. He is a confidant to whom you can tell everything and who helps to reduce anxiety in difficult situations.
François Hugues

Our familiar companions, these "love machines", are consumed by the intensity of the love they give us. The strength of their feelings, of their passion does not agree with a longer life.
Jean-Pierre Hutin

When a dog or cat is already very old, I recommend taking another younger one.
Reha Hutin

When you have long lived with an animal, you finally know it.
Reha Hutin

If you want to write, keep cats.
Aldous Huxley

No man ever dared to manifest his boredom so insolently as does a Siamese tomcat when he yawns in the face of his amorously importunate wife
Aldous Huxley

It was a true alley cat, a leggy, long-headed beast, regularly striated with ebony waves encircling legs with black bracelets, stretching eyes by two big zigzags of ink.
Joris-Karl Huysmans

She waited for him in the hallway at the door, scratching the wood, mewing even before she had whined into the room, then she rolled her languid green gold-eyes, rubbed against his pants, jumped o to the furniture, stood upright, simulating the little rearing horse, gave him, when he approached, great butts of friendship,.
Joris-Karl Huysmans

Cat, I'm a kitty-cat, and I dance, dance, dance, and I dance, dance, dance
Steve Ibsen

A cat who turns her nose up at bread does not deserve meat.
Mehmet Ildan

A cat can be trusted to purr when she is pleased, which is more than can be said for human beings.
William Ralph Inge

Daisy: This is simply a cat run over by a pachyderm, a rhinoceros in this case.
Botard: Maybe it was just a flea crushed by a mouse. We 're making such a to-do about it.
Eugène Ionesco

All cats are mortal, Socrates is mortal, therefore Socrates is a cat.
Eugène Ionesco

An extraordinary earthquake happened in eastern Japan. But, the cat came as usual.
Hajime Irisawa

I can imagine a cat changes himself to a philosopher, but a dog does not.
Hajime Irisawa

Cats are glorious creatures who must on no account be underestimated Their eyes are fathomless depths of cat-world mysteries.
Lesley Anne Ivory

I whose gaze is not so deep as yours
Can I dare to speak of you without betraying you?
Muriel Jack

I can't help it, it's hard for me to trust someone completely who does not like cats.
Edmond Jaloux

The cat's whiskers are lacking in softness, which is why a cat is called a "failine".
Jean-Charles

On the snow, I noticed a brown cat coming out of a side street and walking across the snow. I looked closer and to my surprise, I saw this huge cat was followed by six small brown and white kittens, they all followed the huge pussy forming a perfect line. The cat looked from time to time behind her to see if all babies were there, but her main concern was to reach the door.
Jean-Paul II

The cat and her kittens did not even mew. They knew the authoritative voice of the Anglican bishop.
Jean-Paul II

The cat jumped in front of me and ran up the stairs, followed by her kittens. I looked up and saw a Jesuit priest expel the cats from the steps.
Jean-Paul II

Animals do have a soul.
Jean-Paul II

What can I do? I cannot speak to cats. I speak to the doorman. But there are lots of hungry birds. Maybe they will pick up the crumbs.
Jean-Paul II

A cat's got her own opinion of human beings. She doesn't say much, but can tell you enough to make you anxious not to hear the whole of it.
Jérôme Klapka Jérôme

Let your boat of life be light, packed with only what you need - a homely home and simple pleasures, one or two friends, worth the name, someone to love and someone to love you, a cat, a dog, and a pipe or two, enough to eat and enough to wear, and a little more than enough to drink; for thirst is a dangerous thing.
Jérôme Klapka Jérôme

Hang sorrow, care'll kill a cat.
Ben Jonson

More likely than not, it was a cat who first coined and put into practice the wise piece of advice: 'If you would have a thing done well, you must do it yourself.'
Lawrence N. Johnson

The domestic cat seems to have greater confidence in itself than in anyone else.
Lawrence N. Johnson

When anyone mistreats it, the cat wants nothing more to do with that person and will remember him or her for a long time. It doesn't believe in the doctrine of turning the other cheek and won't pretend that it does.
Lawrence N. Johnson

All cats are possessed of a proud spirit, and the surest way to forfeit the esteem of a cat is to treat him as an inferior being.
Michael Joseph

His friendship is not easily won but it is something worth having.
Michael Joseph

Is it yet another survival of jungle instinct, this hiding away from prying eyes at important times? Or merely a gesture of independence, a challenge to man and his stupid ways?

The cats have taken their existence as a fact of Creation.
Michael Joseph

~~Franz Kafka~~
Franz Kafka

This is not a joke, the rats have taken over the Royal Library and eaten all the books. There is talk of replacing the librarians by cats. - But what will become the modern authors who make new books by copying the old ones?
Alphonse Karr

I cannot deny that a cat lover and his cat have a master/slave relationship. The cat is the master.
Arthur R. Kassin

Myself and a buddy had a rifle and shot a cat, he died only two weeks after...
Mathieu Kassovitz

Cats and mongooses will be used as protection against rats and snakes.
Kautilya (Arthashastra)

In case of danger from rats, grasshoppers, birds or insects, appropriate animals (cats, mongooses) will be released and these predators must be protected against the risk of being killed or attacked by dogs.
Kautilya (Arthashastra)

The daily ration for an Arya man is one prastha of rice, one quarter prastha of bread, one kuduba of oil or butter and one quarter kuduba of salt. For a non-Aryan, a prastha of rice, one sixth prastha of bread, one half-kuduba of oil and one quarter kuduba of salt. [...] For a dog, one prastha of rice.
Kautilya (Arthashastra)

Whoever has stolen or killed a small animal (rooster, cat, dog, pig) of a value under 25 panas will have the nose cut or pay a fine of 54 panas.
Kautilya (Arthashastra)

Turn away your sad, green bright gaze. Prick up your velvety ears, but, please, do not stick your claws in me.
John Keats

Their uncanny intelligence, a strong streak of stubbornness and independence can make it a challenge to show them. If you wish to show a Mau, you must begin early when it is a kitten, getting it acclimatized to the sights and sounds of a cat show, otherwise they may decide they don't like the whole idea of leaving home when they are older. It's their stubbornness coming through!

Dee Keenan

Cats are intended to teach us that not everything in nature has a function.
Garrison Keillor

It is good to look at things from different perspectives. However, never at your exact opposite, that is your reflection in the mirror of whom you will never be the winner. As any cat can tell you.
Frederik Kerling

Women are like cats and dogs. If you can attract any cat and make any dog listen to you, you can have any women you like.
Frederik Kerling

Mewing is like aloha - it can mean anything.
Hank Ketchum

Curiosity killed the cat and information brought it back!
Marian Keyes

He turned his back on me and roared away, like a cat showing me its bum.
Marian Keyes

Cat said, 'I am not a friend, and I am not a Servant. I am the Cat who walks by himself, and I wish to come into your Cave.'
Rudyard Kipling

I am the Cat who walks by himself. I do not agree to anything, but you'll see that you 'll be happy to have me at your home.
Rudyard Kipling

The wildest of all was the Cat. He walked alone and all places were alike to him.
Rudyard Kipling

_ From now on your name is Gally!
_ Hey what... was not that the name of your cat... He who died last month?
Yukito Kishiro

Cats are rather delicate creatures and they are subject to a good many ailments, but I never heard of one who suffered from insomnia.
Joseph Wood Krutch

Cats seem to act on the principle that it never does any harm to ask for what you want.
Joseph Wood Krutch

A dog is like a liberal, he wants to please everybody. A cat doesn't really need to know that everybody loves him.

William Kunstler

A cat never smiles despite the fact that it is what he prefers.

Jean L'Anselme

A man passionately loved his cat;
She was cute, and beautiful, and delicate
And mewed a very mild tone.

Jean de La Fontaine

Four different animals, Grasp -Cheese the Cat,
Sad-Bird the Owl, Gnaw-Mesh the Rat,
Lady Weasel the long bodiced,
All villainous people
Haunted the rotten trunk of an old wild pine.

Jean de La Fontaine

It was a cat living as a devout hermit,
A simpering cat,
A holy man of a cat, well stuffed, big and fat,
A Referee expert in all cases.

Jean de La Fontaine

No favour can win gratitude from a cat.

Jean de La Fontaine

Gnaw-Mesh goes back to Cat, and causes
A link to be undone, then another, and then both.
And finally it releases the hypocrite.

Jean de La Fontaine

The Cat was often irritated by Bird:
One f fought with beak, the other played with paws.

Jean de La Fontaine

The fox finally said to the cat:
"You pretend to be very clever,
Do you know as much as me? I have a hundred tricks in my bag.
_ No, said the other: I have only one in my wallet,
But I maintain that it is worth a thousand. "

Jean de La Fontaine

This flour-covered block looks suspicious to me,
He exclaimed from afar to the Cats' General.

Jean de La Fontaine

This exterminator Cat,
True Cerberus, was feared a league round:
He wanted to depopulate the world from Mice.
           Jean de La Fontaine

You will never be the masters.
Let the door be closed in his face, he will return through the windows.
           Jean de La Fontaine

The dog goes mew mew, the cat goes Wah-Wah.
           Jacques Lacan

Debts are like rats on a ship without a cat... They devours a boat in no time.
           Pierre Djada Lacroix

O my beautiful cold-fearing cat, when gloomy autumn
Makes the kids in courtyards yelp louder
How many did we spend of these spleeny days
Dreaming face to face in my well closed room..
           Jules Laforgue

I put down my book, The Meaning of Zen, and see the cat smiling into her fur as she delicately combs it with her rough pink tongue. Cat, I would lend you this book to study but it appears you have already read it. She looks up and gives me her full gaze. Don't be ridiculous, she purrs, I wrote it.
           Dilys Laing

Egyptian Maus are loving and fiercely loyal companions who want to be at your side and involved in every aspect of your life. They often express their happiness by chortling and trilling in a soft melodious voice and with their tails quivering while treading on their forepaws.
           Peter Lamb

_ Who did this?
_ It is the cat! He watches too much television.
           Nicole Lambert

Cats, like men, are flatterers.
           Walter Savage Landor

Of all animals, the cat alone attains to contemplative life. He regards the wheel of existence from without, like the Buddha.
           Andrew Lang

Whereas we can just about leave our wife or our husband without too much suffering, we will never abandon our cat.

Jacques Lanzmann

The cat obeys only himself. He says no to everything rather than yes perhaps.

Jacques Lanzmann

The cat forces upon us reflection and sentimentality.

Jacques Lanzmann

Understanding a dog is within reach of everyone. His yelps, his attitudes tell as much as a speech. However, understanding a cat is more complex.

Jacques Lanzmann

What fascinates us in the cat is precisely that he is beyond the reach of the clumsy logic of the dog and that hugs and treats are not enough to put him in our pocket.

Jacques Lanzmann

Greg the Egyptian Mau and Betty the Russian Blue both melted my heart when I saw them. I had a hard time deciding which of the two would be my four- legged friend.

Catherine Lara

When arriving, I call to her: "Peggy!" Knock, knock, I hear her little paws on the floor. She comes from my closet, where she sleeps in my sweaters. What a wonderful moment! With Peggy, I've really discovered cat love.

Catherine Lara

*Dumas delighted in maintaining a real menagerie: Caesar the cock, Mysouf the cat, Jugurtha the vulture, not counting the monkeys.
- I hate beasts, he said, but I love animals.*

Lorédan Larcher

The cat could very well be man's best friend but would never stoop to admitting it.

Doug Larson

Just cross your gaze with that of a cat to measure the depth of riddles that every spark of his eyes rouses in the brave humans that we are.

Jacques Laurent

One never chooses a cat: it is he who chooses you.

Jacques Laurent

I am suddenly awakened by a noise... is it... a cat stabbed by a hunting knife? No. No, it is my son, he is hungry and his diaper is so full that I intend to hire a groom soon.

Bill Lawrence

Oh, Auntie, isn't he a beauty! And is he a gentleman or a lady? Neither, my dear! I had him fixed. It saves him from so many undesirable associations.
D. H. Lawrence

Cats, like all animals, like to drink water as cool as possible. Princess Eli-Ora tried to drink directly from the tap. She learned very quickly.
Patrick Le Coustumer

The durian was ripe. This event explained everything, because the smell of the fruit seems to drive men into madness as valerian does with cats.
Henri Le Fauconnier

I turn, O beautiful cat, to your holy pupils, and it seems to me that I have two stars in front of me.
Le Tasse

The Owl and the Pussy-Cat went to sea in a beautiful pea-green boat. They took some honey, and plenty of money, wrapped up in a five-pound note.
Edward Lear

Whenever a mistress leaves me, I adopt an alley cat: an animal leaves, another comes.
Paul Léautaud

I never had a cat like him, smart, attentive, loquacious responsive, knowing what he wanted to ask, following me about in the garden like a dog - and I think I'll never be for any other animal what I have been for him.
Paul Léautaud

We talked tonight, Valette and I, about this scratching of clothes with their hands that all the dying have, or almost all of them. I told him that animals do the same, at least dogs and cats, many of which I saw die. A dog, a cat at the moment of death, if they are on the floor of a garden, scratch the ground with their forepaws, if they are in a house, scratch the floor, if they are on a bed, scratch the bed on which they are. What does this gesture mean, this movement, that both humans and animals share? It probably has the same animal origin, purely instinctive.
Paul Léautaud

It is not luck if you pass beneath a black cat, but hardly anybody knows.
Pierre Legaré

His mind is like a steel trap - full of mice.
Foghorn Leghorn

My cat, sacred host of my old house,
Make round your elastic flexible back,
Come and curl up on my knees, and let
Me slip my hands across your warm hair.

Half Close, a long shudder running across your kidneys,
Your green eye who mocks me, but caresses me,
Your green eye with a touch of gold, charged with laziness,
Watching me in an ironic and benign way.

You never knew, philosopher, oh old brother,
the silly and noisy fidelity of the dog.
You love me, however and my heart does feel it.

Your clear-sighted and perhaps ephemeral love
I like and I salute in you, calm thinker,
Exquisite virtues: skepticism and gentleness.

Jules Lemaître

Cats are living adornments.

Edwin Lent

Here lies a pretty cat
His mistress who loved nothing
Loved her to distraction:
Why say it?
You see it!

Madame de Lesdiguières

Green eyes, so green, but in the shade, of dark and smoked gold - a cat with dark eyes.

Doris Lessing

If a fish is the movement of water embodied, given shape, then a cat is a diagram and pattern of subtle air.

Doris Lessing

It is an elegant cat, with a noble and curved profile, like a grave's cat.

Doris Lessing

The designer of the cat had decided: I will create a black cat, the quintessential black cat, a cat from hell.

Doris Lessing

Cat would be the elephant's god,
If the mouse he ate in front.

Charles de Leusse

A laughing cat is mad.
A man who does not laugh is below anything.
                                                Charles de Leusse

When a dog mews
It's because he eats him.
                                                Charles de Leusse

Excuse me, but I'll get my cats.
                                                Bernard-Henri Lévy

A dog thinks: Hey, these people I live with feed me, love me, provide me with a nice warm, dry house, pet me, and take good care of me... They must be Gods! A cat thinks: Hey, these people I live with feed me, love me, provide me with a nice warm, dry house, pet me, and take good care of me... I must be a God!
                                                Ira Lewis

If there were an invisible cat in that chair, the chair would look empty; but the chair does look empty, therefore there is an invisible cat in it.
                                                Jack Lewis

A cat's name may tell you more about its owners than it does about the cat.
                                                Linda W. Lewis

He was amazed to see that cats had slitted skin just in place of eyes.
                                                Georg Christoph Lichtenberg

Praying to the sun is something forgivable. Everyone looks unintentionally to a bright place, animals do it and what, in a cat or dog, is an involuntary glance toward the light, is in humans called a prayer.
                                                Georg Christoph Lichtenberg

I found out why cats drink out of the toilet. My mother told me it's because the water is cold in there. How did my mother know that?
                                                Wendy Liebman

I care not much for the religion of a man whose dog and cat are not the better for it.
                                                Abraham Lincoln

No matter how much cats fight, there always seem to be plenty of kittens.
                                                Abraham Lincoln

The world has different owners at sunrise... Even your own garden does not belong to you. Rabbits and blackbirds have the lawns; a tortoise-shell cat who never appears in daytime patrols the brick walls, and a golden-tailed pheasant glints his way through the iris spears.

Anne Lindbergh

I saw the most beautiful cat today. It was sitting by the side of the road, its two forepaws neatly and graciously put together. Then it gravely swished around its tail to completely encircle itself. It was so fit and beautifully neat, that gesture, and so self-satisfied, so complacent.
Ann Morrow Lindbergher

The fear of cats is one of those irrational connections that dishonor our understanding.
John Locke

It is incorrect to think that the cat, the proudest and most virtuous of pets, is "false".
Konrad Lorenz

The cat is a wild animal that inhabits the homes of humans.
Konrad Lorenz

If by chance I seated myself to write, she very slyly, very tenderly, seeking protection and caresses, would softly take her place on my knee and follow the comings and goings of my pen -- sometimes effacing, with an unintentional stroke of her paw, lines of whose tenor she disapproved.
Pierre Loti

Sometimes he would get up suddenly to relax,
- In the manner of a cat stretching, she said.
Pierre Loti

It will never be given to any of us to decipher anything in these cuddly little heads that are so lovingly caressed, held and kneaded in our hands.
Pierre Loti

Their waddle, the flexible soft way in which they placed their bare feet, had something of the cat.
Pierre Loti

The Cat's beauty is classical while the Dog' is gothic.
Howard Lovecraft

Dogs are farmers and farmers' animals, cats are gentlemen and gentlemen's animals.
Howard P. Lovecraft

In its flawless grace and superior self-sufficiency I have seen a symbol of the perfect beauty and bland impersonality of the universe itself, objectively considered, and in its air of silent mystery there resides for me all the wonder and fascination of the Unknown.
Howard P. Lovecraft

It is said that in Ulthar, which lies beyond the river Skai, no man may kill a cat; and this I can verily believe as I gaze upon him who sitteth purring before the fire. For the cat is cryptic, and close to strange things which men cannot see. He is the soul of antique Aegyptus, and bearer of tales from forgotten cities in Meroe and Ophir. He is the king of the jungle's lords, and heir to the secrets of hoary and sinister Africa. The Sphinx is his cousin, and he speaks his language; but he is more ancient than the Sphinx, and remembers that which she hath forgotten.
Howard P. Lovecraft

One piece of evidence of the superior dignity of the cat lies in our practice of using the words "cat" and "dog" to qualify a particular behavior or attitude.
Howard P. Lovecraft

Our charming kittens are similar to doric temples, with Ionic columns of which they have the structural harmony and charm raised to a higher level.
Howard P. Lovecraft

We do not own a cat, we bear with it.
Howard P. Lovecraft

We own a dog - he is with us as a slave and inferior because we wish him to be. But we entertain a cat - he adorns our hearth as a guest, fellow-lodger and equal because he wishes to be there. It is no compliment to be the stupidly idolized master of a dog whose instinct it is to idolize, but it is a very distinct tribute to be chosen as the friend and confidant of a cat.
Howard P. Lovecraft

The cat's wisdom is a model because it combines the most intent passion with the calmest indifference. Motionless it plans its leap, and performs it exactly; the strength of its muscles is matched by its relaxation in repose; in sleep it has the abandon of an infant, yet its instinct is ever alert; it can fall without danger because it does not resist; hunting and fighting are games of pure pleasure for it, it hunts with rancor and plays without an object; it is ever ready to attack without animosity, and to defend itself without apprehension; being indifferent to victory, it cannot feel defeat.
Isha de Lubicz

His ability to see at night suggests secret and supernatural powers that arouse jealousy as much as the fear of the unknown.
Jan and Hélène Lühl

All cats have superb furs and each species exhibits a unique pattern, based on spots or stripes, or with spots and stripes, or even with no spots or stripes at all.
Suzan Lumpkin

Household garbage attracts rats and mice. These three elements constitute a reserve of food for feral cats and can form the center of activity of a group.
Suzan Lumpkin

People give their cat a litter for him to bury his excrements. In nature, many species of small felines also bury their excrements. These contain smelling information for other felines, and the fact of burying prevents the message being sent to a large feline that kills small ones. Among domestic cats who were abandoned and became feral cats, the dominant individuals do not bury their excrements, but lower-ranking cats do.
Suzan Lumpkin

In my opinion, one of the pleasures of cats' company is their devotion to bodily comfort.
Sir Compton Mackenzie

Nobody who is not prepared to spoil cats will get from them the reward they are able to give to those who do spoil them.
Sir Compton Mackenzie

The only mystery about the cat is why it ever decided to become a domestic animal.
Sir Compton MacKenzie

People who belong to Siamese cats must make up their minds to do a good deal of waiting upon them.
Sir Compton Mackenzie

There is no harm in forgetting for an hour or two the problems of poverty and children.
And forgetting the heat and flies…
And forgetting there is another world outside these bars…
And enjoying playing with a black cat.
Naguib Mahfouz

The cat blinks. She has waited a long time for you to remember her name. Her purr, steady as the clock's heartbeat, is a bridge from the place you have left to the place where you now are. A reliable companion, she guides you towards the land whose name comes to your lips slowly.
Lisa Suhair Majaj

The modern Egyptian domestic cat, which one encounters in the cafes and bazaars, in the noisy streets of Cairo and in the dusty sun-drenched villages, is a graceful delicate little creature, usually much smaller than Western cats.
Jarovir Malek

Cats are creatures made for storing caresses.
Stéphane Mallarmé

How many long days I spent alone with my cat!
Stéphane Mallarmé

I have a lovely white lady called Snow. It is a pretty breed cat, and I embrace her all day on her pink nose. She wipes out my lines with her tail, walking around the table while I write.
Stéphane Mallarmé

My cat is a mystical companion, a spirit.
Stéphane Mallarmé

My partner became increasingly perplexed. He began playing cat and mouse.
André Malraux

When I am ready to work, the cat jumps off the desk and settles on my white sheet. You ask me how I can write? The fact is I write around the cat.
André Malraux

We are starting to suffer over here, we delight in horse meat, the donkey is overpriced, there are dog butchers, cat butchers and rat butchers - Paris is deadly sad, when will it all end?
Edouard Manet

Maus have an unusual fascination with water. Turn on the faucet or shower, and they are right there trying to catch the water. After flushing the toilet, you quickly learn to keep the seat down!
Dot Mardulier

He drew back to the wall, with narrowed eyes, nodding his head and blowing like an angry cat.
Roger Martin du Gard

I gave my cat a bath the other day... They love it. He sat there, he enjoyed it, it was fun for me. The fur would stick to my tongue, but other than that...
Steve Martin

Cats do not have to be shown how to have a good time, for they are unfailingly ingenious in that respect.

The cat does not negotiate with the mouse.
James Mason

I live in my cats' home and I pay the rent.
Robert K. Massie

He is at home everywhere, able to come in everywhere, the animal that passes across without a noise, the silent stalker, the night walker of hollow walls.
Bruno Masure

Nothing is sweeter, nothing gives the skin a sensation more delicate, more refined, more rare than the warm vibrant fur of a cat.
Guy de Maupassant

I love the intense deep emptiness of his glaze, the intense empty depth of his eyes, this plenitude of nothing which is perhaps the unknown.
Guy de Maupassant

Claude Mauriac

The acorn becomes an oak through automatic growth; no commitment is necessary. The kitten similarly becomes a cat out of pure instinct. Nature and being are identical in creatures like them. But a man or woman becomes fully human only by his or her choices and his or her commitment to them. People attain worth and dignity by the multitude of decisions they make from day to day. These decisions require courage.
Rollo May

A cat can purr its way out of anything.
Donna McCrohan

When your cat rubs the side of its face along your leg, it's affectionately marking you with its scent, identifying you as its private property, saying, in effect, 'You belong to me'.
Susan McDonough

The sun rose slowly, like a fiery fur ball coughed up uneasily onto a sky-blue carpet by a giant unseen cat.
Michael McGarel

Men need four things: food, shelter, a pussy and a strange pussy.
Jay McInernay

If there is one spot of sun spilling onto the floor, a cat will find it and soak it up.
Joan Asper McIntosh

A mew massages the heart.
Stuart McMillan

One of the oldest human needs is having someone to wonder where you are when you don't come home at night.
Margaret Mead

The cat has too much spirit to have no heart.
Ernest Menaul

Women do not like timid men. Cats do not like prudent rats.
H.L. Mencken

He falls in love with all cats in hats, imagines that it's forever, then forgets about it after two days.
Prosper Mérimée

Abyssinian is not a cat. He is THE cat.
Joseph Méry

Are cats lazy? Well, more power to them if they are. Which one of us has not entertained the dream of doing just as he likes, when and how he likes, and as much as he likes?
Fernand Mery

You must know your cat better if you want to understand it better.
Fernand Mery

With their qualities of cleanliness, discretion, affection, patience, dignity, and courage, how many of us, I ask you, would be capable of becoming cats?
Fernand Mery

God created the cat for man to have the pleasure of caressing the tiger.
Joseph Méry

Cats are smart. You know it and I know it.
Debbie Mertens

Some animals are secretive; some are shy. A cat is private.
Leonard Michaels

There is no evidence that the flea that lives on mice fears cats.
Henri Michaux

A dog will flatter you but you have to flatter the cat.
George Mikes

You can keep a dog; but it is the cat who keeps people, because cats find humans useful domestic animals.
George Mikes

When I raise a cat from kittenhood, it learns to read me so well that it can con me and predict what I'm going to do. A young adult cat doesn't know

what to expect from me and I don't know what to expect from it, so we immediately have each other's attention.
Karl Lewis Miller

Cats regard people as warm-blooded furniture.
Jacquelyn Mitchard

You spoke about dogs and cats, I too love them very much. Besides, I think we have dogs of the same race, God knows how much we get attached... But you do not have the monopoly of the heart of dogs and cats.
François Mitterrand

Drenching the pavement, warming the wall, bathing the cat in a slumbering sprawl... Waking the buds that break from the tree. Shaking out gold, and all for free.
Tony Mitton

We cannot, unless we become cats, perfectly understand the cat's mind.
St. George Mivart

Cats are not impure; they keep watch about us.
The Prophet Mohammed

Kittens believe that all nature is occupied with diverting them.
F.A. Paradis de Moncrif

In a distant age when the seas were only mud hills and mountains, God formed the first man and first woman from clay and let a cat and a dog to watch over them when he left to find the water of eternal life in sources of immortality. In his absence, a demon beguiled heir vigilance by providing milk and meat and, while they paid no attention, he urinated on the new creation of God. The latter, enraged to see the fur of his work so sullied, ordered the cat to clean it with his tongue, except the hair that was intact. The rough tongue of the cat took off all the dirty hair she could reach, leaving only a few in the armpits and groin. God put everything that the cat had removed on the dog. Then he sprinkled his creatures of clay with the sacred waters of the eternal fountain but could not give them immortality because of the desecration the devil had caused.
Mythologie Mongole

When the tea is brought in at five o'clock
And all the neat curtains are drawn with care,
The little black cat with bright green eyes
Suddenly starts purring there.
Harold Monro

The animal can unlock the inner world of the child.
Hubert Montagner

When I play with my cat, who knows if I am not a pastime to her more than she is to me?
Michel Eyquem de Montaigne

Do not marry, do not take holy orders. Do not leave for Africa. Buy a cat.
Henry de Montlherlant

At night all cats are grey.
Montluc

In my next life, I'd like to come back as a cat.
Patti J. Moran

In Memphis, a woman had all the more claims to beauty as she looked like a cat.
Paul Morand

I had at least a hundred cats, or rather, as Michelet said, a hundred cats got me.
Paul Morand

I like cats because they are silent and, as such, misunderstood.
Paul Morand

If someone happened to kill a cat, even accidentally, the Egyptian people would throw themselves on the murderer and make him die under torture.
Paul Morand

Scandinavians made the cat into the emblem of love.
Paul Morand

In Paris it is there that true sanctuaries of cats are located: they are the lodges of concierges.
Paul Morand

Suddenly everything changed: The cat spoke. I mean that, turning his head and looking me in the eyes, he let out a long expressive mew, pathetic and reasonable at the same time.
Alberto Moravia

The playful kitten with its pretty little tigerish gambol is infinitely more amusing than half the people one is obliged to live with in the world.
Lady Sydney Morgan

People with insufficient personalities are fond of cats. These people adore being ignored.
Henry Morgan

They are shoulder riders, refrigerator vultures, and AM "kissers" (furry alarm-clocks with warm raspy tongues.)
Melanie Morgan

His amiable amber eyes
Are very friendly, very wise;
Like Buddha, grave and fat,
He sits, regardless of applause,
And thinking, as he kneads his paws,
What fun to be a cat!"
Christopher Morley

Artists like cats; soldiers like dogs.
Desmond Morris

For the sensitive man, it's a privilege to share a room with a cat, crossing his eyes, feeling it rub against his legs.
Desmond Morris

On tiptoe, he moves in the room, like a cat with velvet paws.
Claude-Aimé Motongane

That night, a cat was mewing near our barbed wire.
Benito Mussolini

She rages like the goddess Sekhmet and she is friendly like the goddess Bastet.
The Myth of the Eye of the Sun

That's firefighters: they save your life, and then they sell you calendars with kittens.
Naguy

The trouble with a kitten is that eventually it becomes a cat.
Ogden Nash

The beasts of the desert shall drink from the river of Egypt and rest on its bank because nobody shall scare them away.
The Profecies of Nefertiti

Winners are different. They're a different breed of cat.
Byron Nelson

Cats do care. For example they know instinctively what time we have to be at work in the morning and they wake us up twenty minutes before the alarm goes off.
Michael Nelson

A cat holds carefully between his sharp teeth a piece of fish studded with bones: swallow it would frighten him, spit it would give him regrets.
Irène Némirovsky

*I have seen
How the cat trembles
while sleeping
The night runs over him
like dark water*
Pablo Neruda

I would gladly change places with any of my cats.
George Ney

I think I'll come back as a cat.
George Ney

A garden without cats, it will be generally agreed, can scarcely deserve to be called a garden at all.
Beverly Nichols

Man wishes woman to be peaceable, but in fact she is essentially warlike, like the cat.
Friedrich Nietzsche

Most of us rather like our cats to have a streak of wickedness. I should not feel quite easy in the company of any cat that walked about the house with a saintly expression
Beverly Nichols

A cat is a puzzle for which there is no solution.
Hazel Nicholson

My cat and I have an agreement: I leave her alone and don't make sudden moves when I wake up to find her perched on my chest, staring with an unblinking hostile gaze at my face and in return she rarely mutilates me.
James Nicoll

Perhaps a child, like a cat, is so much inside himself that he does not see himself in the mirror.
Anais Nin

Cats like doors to be left open - in case they change their minds.
Rosemary Nisbet

It was noticed that among all animals, women, flies and cats are those who spend more time grooming.
Charles Nodier

Always the cat remains a little beyond the limits we try to set for him in our blind folly.
André Norton

Thou shalt have thy house with blue tiles, hydrangeas in casements, palms trees in skies, crackling winters near the Angora cat.
Claude Nougaro

Another superiority of cat on man: he does not speak.
Louis Nucera

Loving cats is to be on the right side once and for all, it is abolishing the old superstitions, it is rehabilitating the heretics.
Louis Nucera

The cat does not promise, that saves him from reversing his judgment.
Louis Nucera

The refusal of cats to understand is deliberate.
Louis Nucera

The superiority of the cat on man is undeniable.
Louis Nucera

There are beauties that are beyond words. Cats belong to this order.
Louis Nucera

Not speaking, the cat does not betray any secrets.
Louis Nucera

Love plays with my heart as a cat plays with a mouse.
Abu Nuwas

The white cat on the white chair lives white minutes I'm not even in.
Naomi Shihab Nye

Cats possess so many of the same qualities as some people that it is often hard to tell people and cats apart.
P. J. O'Rourke

It is easy to understand why the cat has eclipsed the dog as modern America's favorite pet. People like pets to possess the same qualities that they do. Cats are irresponsible and recognize no authority, yet are completely dependent on others for their material needs. Cats cannot be made to do anything useful. Cats are mean for the fun of it. In fact, cats possess so many of the same qualities as some people that it is often hard to tell people and cats apart.
P.J. O'Rourke

Cats are like paper, they are very quickly hurt.

René de Obaldia

The Game of Cat. - It was another allegory. A Jew had a pole surmounted by the golden calf and three others, one having a cat in hand, bowed before the idol. Entered Moses with the tablets of the law, his face marked by great anger; the high priest Aaron, dressed in his pontifical robes, trying to calm his anger. Finally the one who carried the cat threw it into the air, a circumstance from which the game took its name. It is this animal, adored in Egypt, that brought the Israelites to idolatry of the golden calf. Here, the action of throwing it into the air meant that Moses received the submission of the Israelites, who gave up the superstitions of Egypt.

Henri Oddo

Cats soothe the soul. Cats have no worries, because they think intuitively.
Pal Gerhard Olsen

To wake the sleeping cat.
Charles d'Orléans

The mathematical probability of a common cat doing exactly as it pleases is the one scientific absolute in the world.
Lynn M. Osband

Any member introducing a dog into the Society's premises shall be liable to a fine of one pound. Any animal leading a blind person shall be deemed to be a cat.
Oxford Union Society

The cat lets Man support her. But unlike the dog, she is no handlicker. Furthermore, unlike Man's other great good friend, the horse, the cat is no sweating serf of Man. The only labor she condescends to perform is to catch mice and rats, and that's fun.
Vance Packard

Ah? There you are, you? Look, here she is, the Pomponnette... you bitch, bitch, Now it is that you come back? And poor Pompon, say, who was worried sick all these three days! He kept pacing up and down, he looked everywhere... More unhappy than a stone he was... And, all that time with her alley cat... A stranger, a bum... a moonlight passer-by.
Marcel Pagnol

Our character is what God and cats know of us.
Thomas Paine

The last thing I would accuse a cat of is innocence.
Edward Paley

A baited cat may grow as fierce as a lion.

Samuel Palmer

The reader is as ungrateful as a cat. The cat, who is a very intelligent animal, is not ungrateful, but he knows he should not rely on writers who love only dogs. Do not get concerned about cats or dogs, but about the country's problems.

Orhan Pamuk

It's a bad guy who kicks off the cats!

Christopher Paolini

Her skin was the color of blond honey, her face that of a cat, and she moved with grace, flexibility and power that reflected her ease in battle and her natural strength.

Christopher Paolini

The elf was magnificent in action, a perfect blend of control and indomitable violence. She leaped like a cat, hit like a heron, tacked and cavorted with the grace of a weasel.

Christopher Paolini

Cats have uncommon personalities.

Christopher Paolini

Suddenly a pair of eyes appeared, glowing in the dark. A moment later a huge cat jumped on to the counter. His body was thin but muscular, and his claws seemed enormous. A shaggy mane haloed his angular face. His ears were dotted with black tufts. Under his coat, one guessed a powerful jaw.

Christopher Paolini

Kittens believe that all nature is occupied with diverting them.

F.A. Paradis de Moncrif

You may not, cannot, appropriate beauty. It is the wealth of the eye, and a cat may gaze upon a king.

Theodore Parker

Animals are the small part of God's creation, and one day we shall meet them again in the mystery of Christ.

Paul VI

You cannot look at a sleeping cat and feel tense.

Jane Pauley

A dog is a dog, a bird is a bird, and a cat is a person.

Mugsy Peabody

There is nothing to understand or expect from us. Because we are not of your world. Do you know how to talk to dogs, cats, earthworms?
Pierre Pelot

Sleeping together is a euphemism for people, but tantamount to marriage with cats.
Marge Percy

You can be the God of dogs, the God of cats, the God of the poor, you just need a leash, some slack, some fortune, but you'll never be the master of a tree. All you can do is want to become a tree in your turn.
Georges Perec

*With the letters of his name,
The French dog builds his house:
Chien (dog) / niche (kennel);
However this is not the case
For the cat
Who has not a house of his own,
Except alleys!
And alleys
Filled with rats:
That's not very inviting!*
Domi Perez

A cat will do what it wants when it wants, and there's not a thing you can do about it.
Frank Perkins

Cats conspire to keep us at arm's length.
Frank Perkins

The cat became a great lord, and never again ran after a mouse but for playing.
Charles Perrault

A giddy young rabbit jumped into his bag and master cat pulling the strings at once took him and killed him.
Charles Perrault

Whenever I see a cat in the sun, I think of humanity.
Fernando Pessoa

The way to get on with a cat is to treat it as an equal - or even better, as the superior it knows itself to be.
Elizabeth Peters

Go away, I love only good cats!

Peyo

A cat pours his body on the floor like water. It is restful just to see him.
William Lyon Phelps

Bossuet said masses for animals.
Monseigneur Dominique Philippe

When I started to bless animals, they called me crazy.
Monseigneur Dominique Philippe

You cannot have a better life than cats: they do what they want, when they want, as much as they want.
Ricardo Philips

God is really only another artist. He invented the giraffe, the elephant and the cat. He has no real style, he just goes on trying other things.
Pablo Picasso

I want to create a cat like the real cats I see crossing the streets, not like those you see in houses. They have nothing in common. The cat of the streets has bristling fur. It runs like a fiend, and if it looks at you, you think it is going to jump in your face.
Pablo Picasso

Brindon asked me what I had made of the wounded cat and I just told him I had changed him into a bird. "If you did, then turn me into a goat," he said jokingly.
Robert Pinget

If the cat takes possession of the sheet while his master is busy covering it with words, let the latter give in. This is a sign that what he had written wasn't worth much and that what was to come would have been worse.
Bernard Pivot

Managing senior programmers is like herding cats.
Dave Platt

Cats, too, with what silent stealthiness, with what light steps do they creep up to a bird!
Pline l'Ancien

It is told that in a cat's eyes, pupils fill and expand at full moon and contract on the wane of this star.
Plutarque

This cat was a remarkably strong and beautiful animal, entirely black, and of wonderful sagacity. Speaking of his intelligence, my wife, who at heart was not a little imbued with superstition, made frequent allusions to the ancient belief that regarded all black cats as witches in disguise.
Edgar Allan Poe

I wish I could write as mysteriously as a cat.
Edgar Allan Poe

I call a cat a cat and Rolet an impostor.
Jean-Baptiste Poquelin (Molière)

The little cat is dead.
Jean-Baptiste Poquelin (Molière)

To pull the chestnuts out of the fire with the cat's paw.
Jean-Baptiste Poquelin (Molière)

It's funny how dogs and cats know the inside of folks better than other folks do, isn't it?
Eleanor H. Porter

If cats could talk, they wouldn't.
Nan Porter

The problem with cats is that they have got exactly the same look whether they see a moth or a murderer with an axe.
Paula Poundstone

Every contented cat was worshipped like a god. He has never forgotten it.
Helen Powers

You can tell your cat anything and he'll still love you. If you lose your job or your best friend, your cat will think no less of you.
Helen Powers

"I meant", said Ipslore bitterly, "what is there in this world that truly makes living worth while?" Death thought about it "Cats", he said eventually, "Cats are nice".
Terry Pratchett

In ancient times, cats were worshiped as gods. They have never forgotten this.
Terry Pratchett

A village listens in sorrow The song of a wounded bird
This is the only bird in the village
And that's the only cat in the village
Who has half eaten it.
Jacques Prévert

You became wild, you became an alley cat!
Don't you fly around my heart like a nightingale?
Nizar Qabbani

Don't wake the sleeping cat.
Rabelais

They pissed everywhere!
Jean Racine

What appears as a dream to others, more gullible, seemed to me as real as the cheese to the cat, despite the bell jar. Yet the bell exists.
Raymond Radiguet

You never choose a cat: he chooses you.
Philippe Ragueneau

In reality, cats are probably better off remaining indoors and sending out their humans to deal with the outside world.
Dr. Phyllis Sherman Raschke

Dawn runs on the heels of the night, like a cat on those of a mouse.
Jean Ray

To go like a cat upon a hot bakestone.
Jean Ray

It is widely acknowledged that cats are akin to hackers.
Eric S. Raymond

To him, musical compositions from Talus strongly resembled the cries of two sand cats trapped in a bag.
Michael Reaves

Cats often devise their own sets of rules that they think we should live by, and they may be quick to chastise us if we fail to adhere to these rules!
Margaret Reister

He knows a cat, despised because he is old, sick, and hairless here and there.
Jules Renard

I'm sure the cat does not think; yet it looks as deep as if he thought.
Jules Renard

A cat who sleeps twenty hours a day is perhaps God's best achievement.
Jules Renard

She is told: "catch mice and leave birds!" This is very subtle and the sharpest cat may be mistaken.
Jules Renard

The ideal of calm exists in a sitting cat.
Jules Renard

Then she told me, "instead of alienating yourself
With this damn useless TV,
Listen, your kid 's just woken up.

Go and heat his bottle
And, if it's not asking too much,
Will you change the litter of the cat... "
Renaud

Cats are misunderstood, maligned, slandered by ignorant people who thus often give the full measure of their selfishness or wickedness.
Marcel Reney

A kitten is chiefly remarkable for rushing about like mad at nothing whatever, and generally stopping before it gets there.
Agnès Repplier

A kitten is the most irresistible comedian in the world. Its wide-open eyes gleam with wonder and mirth. It darts madly at nothing at all, and then, as though suddenly checked in the pursuit, prances sideways on its hind legs with ridiculous agility and zeal.
Agnes Repplier

It is impossible for a lover of cats to banish these alert, gentle, discriminating little friends, who give us just enough of their regard and complaisance to make us hunger for more.
Agnes Repplier

The human race may be divided into people who love cats and people who hate them; the neutrals being few in numbers, and, for intellectual and moral reasons, not worth considering.
Agnès Repplier

People that hate cats will come back as mice in their next life.
Faith Resnick

He just took the most abandoned pose, now extending its claws now drawing them back into their velvet sheath, closing its eyes and slightly opening them with a look of bliss, singing this particular murmur that our language can evoke only by imitating it poorly, and which suggests that the perfect rest of the body, mind and heart can lead to the sweetest and most desirable condition.
Reynard cycle

Tibert the Cat: But do not forget it another time, cheats never win.
Reynard cycle

And you find there, unexpected, your glaze
In the amber of the round stones
Of its eyes: prisoner
Like an insect dead since immemorial time.
Rainier Maria Rilke

I do not know what purpose the Creation had when making the cat. An aesthetic success, like the horse? A thing of beauty linked to a certain eroticism?

Angelo Rinaldi

The cat does not caress us, she caresses herself against us.

Rivarol

It's a nice game, playing off-ground tag! But why not off-ground cat?

Roba (Boule et Bill)

I do not understand, Mr. Teacher, there is a total idiot who has imitated the cat's mew and the dog thought it was you!

Roba (Boule et Bill)

He affected a deep contempt for t dogs, because he thought they were subservient and groveling, and great respect for cats, because he thought they had a more open temper, and no less attachment.

Roderer

And when the fur shelters a fatty flesh, it is fine forms in a velvet gown, woman, snake, monkey and dove through grace.

Maurice Rollinat

The cat, however clean he is, though already well-combed, preens himself with great care.

Maurice Rollinat

Home panther, miniature tiger, I like you for your vagueness and your amenity.

Maurice Rollinat

His company brings the lonely man the comforting balm of mysticism.

Maurice Rollinat

The cat has a prophetic spirit and ancient Egyptians were right in honouring it.

Pierre de Ronsard

The cat in gloves catches no mice.

Franklin Delano Roosevelt

Caresses never turned a tiger into a kitten.

Franklin Delano Roosevelt

It is a small black cat, cheeky as a page.
I let it play on my table, often.
Sometimes he sits down without making a fuss;
Looking like a nice paperweight alive.

Edmond Rostand

His eyes, yellow and blue, are like two agates;
He closes them half, sometimes, while sniffing,
Overturns, having seized his nose between his paws,
Looking somehow like a tiger lying on its side.
Edmond Rostand

When you are a cat, you are the one that goes alone and for which all paths are identical.
Jacques Roubaud

When you are a cat, you are a cat. When you are a cat you are not a dog.
Jacques Roubaud

Subtle combination of grace, elegance and power, this cat with his legendary past will fill you with his tenderness, his softness and his unlimited faithfulness.
You will be stunned by the surprising contrast between his coat naturally spotted, short and glossy and his bright green eyes.
Marylène Roulier

It seduces us with his grace and beauty, and his movements are elegant, smooth and precise. His glaze fascinates, and so does this hieratic immobility that can turn in a few tenths of a second into power and violence, making the sleeper into a formidable hunter.
Pierre Rousselet-Blanc

The conquest of Khwarezm by Genghis Khan: we are talking about hundreds of thousands of victims, the killing of any living thing, including dogs and cats - but artisans and priests of all religions are saved.
Jean-Paul Roux

It was either a very big cat, or a little tiger.
Joanne K. Rowling

He blinked his eyes and stared at the cat. The latter stared him back.
Joanne K. Rowling

He noticed an unusual detail: a cat reading a map.
Joanne K. Rowling

I've never seen a cat standing so stiff.
You too would be a bit stiff if you sat all day on a brick wall.
Joanne K. Rowling

The cat merely looked at him with a stern gaze.
Joanne K. Rowling

The whole house smelled of cabbage and Mrs. Figgs spent his time showing him pictures of all the cats she had had.

Joanne K. Rowling

A cat is rarely enthusiastic. A dog is, too often. A man, too.
Claude Roy

Even if you have just destroyed a Ming Vase, purr. Usually it will all be forgiven.
Lenny Rubenstein

Each one of our cats is a distinct, four-footed little person with an individual personality.
Ira B. Rubin

Rosebuds surrounded by thorns: Mother cat carrying babies in her mouth.
Rita Rudner

Cats are a waste of fur.
Jalaluddin Rumi

The Prophet put his noble hand on the forehead of the cat and that is why every cat has four dark lines on her forehead.
Jalaluddin Rumi

Snake slipped into a mosque, "I'm flying from an enemy, protect me." Hedgehog said, "Give me my prey so I can eat." He was given a liver instead.
Snake twisted around the mosque guard intending to bite him. Another person came to help with a bag with a cat inside it.
The Prophet stroked the cat on its back for killing the snake, and doing so, blessed it.
This is why the cat lands on its feet - the cat's back, because of the Prophet's touching it, can never hit the ground.
Jalaluddin Rumi

It's a new fashion: everybody poses nude in calendars! What a change! Until now, we had the choice between kittens in Post Office calendars and big pussies in calendars for truck drivers!
Laurent Ruquier

The first ad to make TV attractive to cats! Usually in ads it's mainly pussies that are shown because that appeals to men.
Laurent Ruquier

The Black Cat protects home and family from superstition.
Laurent Ruquier

If you do not know how to recognize good from bad pork tongue in jelly, throw it in the cat towel!
Laurent Ruquier

A third of abandoned cats are black cats.
Laurent Ruquier

Dangling punch lines to forgotten stories remains in the language like the smile of the Cheshire cat.
William Safire

Though ensuring the triumph of the cat, the tortured mouse must mimic indifference. These are the refinements of civilized life.
Paule Saint-Onge

Confront a child, a puppy, and a kitten with a sudden danger; the child will turn instinctively for assistance, the puppy will grovel in abject submission, the kitten will brace its tiny body for frantic resistance.
Saki (H. H. Munro)

He seems the incarnation of everything soft and silky and velvety, without a sharp edge in his composition, a dreamer whose philosophy is sleep and let sleep.
Saki (H. H. Munro)

The cat is domestic only as far as suits its own ends...
Saki (H. H. Munro)

The cat of the slums and alleys, starved, outcast, harried,... still displays the self-reliant watchfulness which man has never taught it to lay aside.
Saki (H. H. Munro)

I call a cat a pussy
San Antonio

You may own a cat, but cannot govern one.
Kate Sanborn

When addressed, a gentleman cat does not move a muscle. He looks as if he hadn't heard.
Mary Sarton

When you want to hold a cat that was injured, he scratches and runs away.
Marcelle Sauvageot

*My cat has got no name
We simply call him Cat;
He doesn't seem to blame
Anyone for that.*

*For he is not like us
Who often, I'm afraid,*

*Kick up quite a fuss
If our names are mislaid.*
Vernon Scannell

However, the wild cat did not return; the Lady is furious, less for the pearls from her neck than for the loss of the Tomcat.
Paul Scarron

Cats do not like anything that seems to appear as subjection and they prize the independence in which they are born.
Paul Scarron

Cats speak a subtle language in which few sounds carry many meanings, depending on how they are sung or purred. 'Mnrhnh' means comfortable soft chairs. It also means fish. It means genial companionship... and the absence of dogs.
Val Schaffner

When British naturalist E. W. Lane lived in Cairo in the 1830s he was quite amazed to see, every afternoon, a great number of cats gathering in the garden of the High Court, where people would bring baskets full of food for them. In this way, he was told, the qadi fulfilled obligations dating from the thirteen century-rule of the Mamluk sultan, al-Zahir Baybars,
Anne-Marie Schimmel

As surely as the cat begins to purr when you stroke his back, as surely we see a sweet ecstasy painted on the figure of the man you praise, especially when the praise is about the scope of his claims, even though it might be a palpable lie.
Arthur Schopenhauer

He who is cruel to animals cannot be a good man.
Arthur Schopenhauer

Because of our willingness to accept cats as superhuman creatures, they are the ideal animals with which to work creatively.
Roni Schotter

*_ This cartoon cat, where is he coming from?
_ He resumed his office today after a month's layoff. You shut up?
_ You, listen a little to what I 'm saying? A cartoon cat has just entered your office! Ooh ooh!
_ And he 'll still be there tomorrow! We aren't gonna spend Christmas Eve over that!
_ This cat is one of my best men! What's that gnome? Why does he laugh like that?*
Arnold Schwartzenegger

There are two sorts of refuge from the miseries of life: music and cats.
Albert Schweitzer

Cats are a mysterious kind of folk. There is more passing in their minds than we are aware of.
Walter Scott

Cats are lucky: darkness does not prevent them from reading.
Louis Scutenaire

Mice are not superstitious because they know very well that they can also be eaten by a white cat.
Patrick Sébastien

Once the cats that had not the tip of their tail cut used to assemble at a fixed date.
Paul Sébillot

Cats mewed angrily, vaulted their soft back whose hair bristled, straightened their tail and looked at him with eyes that glowed in the night.
Paul Sébillot

Cats are even more curious than girls.
Joann Sfar (the Rabbi's Cat)

Even a kitten would not believe such stupidities.
Joann Sfar (the Rabbi's Cat)

As for Jews, they don't like dogs. A dog, that bites you, that chases you, that barks at you. And it's been so long that the Jews have been bitten, chased or barked over that, finally, they prefer cats.
Joann Sfar (the Rabbi's Cat)

If cats could talk, they would tell some amazing things.
Joann Sfar (the Rabbi's Cat)

In Jewish tradition, the dog is a good pet because he is frank, opinionated, quick to endure suffering for the common good. While the cat, pff! You cannot trust a cat.
Joann Sfar (the Rabbi's Cat)

The human hand is a too subtle a tool to hit people or cats with.
Joann Sfar (the Rabbi's Cat)

The other cats have little conversation.
Joann Sfar (the Rabbi's Cat)

The Torah speaks more of humans than of cats or dogs.
Joann Sfar (the Rabbi's Cat)

There once were two men who went to a judge about a mother cat and her kitten which they both claimed to be theirs. The judge demanded that this cat be set free between their two houses and, depending on which one of the houses she chose, the chosen house would be her master's. And all the people got excited, and I got excited with them. But the cat did not go to either house.

Imam Shafi'i

Thrice the brinded cat hath mewed.

William Shakespeare

I am as vigilant as a cat to steal cream.

William Shakespeare

I could endure anything before but a cat, and now he's a cat to me.

William Shakespeare

My sister crying, our maid howling, our cat wringing her hands.

William Shakespeare

The cat will mew, and dog will have his day.

William Shakespeare

The cat, with eyes of burning coal,
Now Couches 'fore the mouse's hole.

William Shakespeare

What, courage, man! What though care killed a cat, thou hast mettle enough in thee to kill care.

William Shakespeare

What do you want from me,
Good God of cats?
Nothing but one of your nine lives.

William Shakespeare

Many of us are like the little boy we met trudging along a country road with a cat-rifle over his shoulder. What are you hunting, buddy? we asked. Dunno, sir, I ain't seen it yet.

R. Lee Sharpe

Man is civilized to the extent that he understands the cat.

Georges Bernard Shaw

One cat built a secret nest in my socks.
One sat in the window staring up at the street all day while we were at school.
One cat loved the radio dial.
One cat almost smiled

Naomi Shibab Nye

Cats don't adopt people. They adopt refrigerators.

Solomon Short

The cat, when they let him out alone to do his business, never crossed the invisible line that separated the road from the dead-end.
Georges Simenon

Cats are ready to share their lives with humans as long as they can retain some freedom and some independence: they are thus distinguished from other pets. That is why some people love them and others hate them.
Hans Silvester

Often we see cats back from the harbour with a fish in their mouths, sometimes still alive.
Hans Silvester

The words have... this prodigious power to reconcile and confront what but for them would remain scattered... A pin, a parade, a bus line, a plot, a clown, a cat.
Claude Simon

For every house is incomplete without him, and a blessing is lacking in the spirit.
Christopher Smart

Everything I know I learned from my cat: When you're hungry, eat. When you're tired, nap in a sunbeam. When you go to the vet's, pee on your owner.
Gary Smith

The Behaviour of men to animals and their behaviour to each other bear a constant relationship.
Herbert Spencer

In my next life I want to come back as one of my cats. They basically pretend we don't exist. They sit like two bumps on a log and watch us work for hours in the yard. They're probably wondering, along with the entire neighborhood, why we work so hard in our garden and it still looks like hell.
Annie Spiegelman

Who needs television when you have cats?
Lori Spigelmyer

Nothing is improved by anger, unless it be the arch of a cat's back.
Charles Haddon Spurgeon

Since each of us is blessed with only one life, why not live it with a cat?
Robert Stearns

God created man only to serve the cat, to be his slave until the end of time.

All is well that ends well in the world of cats.
Jacques Sternberg

My cat speaks sign language with her tail.
Jacques Sternberg

Among animals, cats are the top-hated, frock-coated statesmen going about their affairs at their own pace.
Robert A. Stern

My name is Steven but they call me Cat.
Robert A. Stern

You can give an order to a dog. To a cat, you can at most make a reasonable proposal.
Cat Stevens

It is in the nature of cats to do a certain amount of unescorted roaming.
Michael Stevens

The cat, the rat, and Lovell the dog. All England is governed by a pig.
Adlai Stevenson

Robert Louis Stevenson

When Mother Nature saw fit to remove the tail of the Manx, she left, in place of the tail, more cat.
Mary E. Stewart

I don't mind a cat, in its place. But its place is not right in the middle of my back at 4 a.m.
Maynard Good Stoddard

I have a good way to judge my employers: they are civilized if they have a cat on the sofa and a little bear on the bed.
Concha Suares

The artist is uncomfortable with his success and with the blizzard of fan mail it has produced. Kliban's recent collections have been conspicuously empty of cats. Cats are wonderful, Kliban once said. It's drawings of cats I 'm getting tired of.
J. C. Suares

When a cat is at the entrance to the rat hole, ten thousand rats do not venture to come out, when a tiger guards the ford, ten thousand deer can cross it.
Sun Tzu

And when I see a cat go I say: He knows a lot about man.
Jules Supervielle

You can't own a cat. The best you can do is be partners.
Sir Harry Swanson

I know Sir John will go, though he was sure it would rain cats and dogs.
Jonathan Swift

Your velvet paw, when we're together,
Know how to touch my hand and make me understand
The price of a friendship able to choose.
Charles S. Swinburne

These enigmatic animals have in their eyes the depth and stars of a piece of sky.
Armand Sylvestre

It is in their eyes that their magic resides.
Arthur Symons

A metaphysician is a man who, at midnight, goes without light in a dark cellar in search of a black cat that is not there.
Charles Synge

She has bewitched me with her darkness and light as she appears to be made of ebony and ivory.
Ibn Tabataba

In your quiet heart and your wide eyes,
O venerable cat, wisdom is innate.
Hippolyte Taine

I have studied many philosophers and many cats. The wisdom of cats is infinitely superior.
Hippolyte Taine

The jinn can take a human or an animal form such as a cow, a scorpion, a snake, a bird... The black dog is the devil of dogs and jinns often appear in this form. They can also appear as a black cat because in fact black adds to the negative force of the devils.
Ibn Taymiya

Dogs eat. Cats dine.
Ann Taylor

Snow falls in cats' paws.
Sylvain Tesson

Cats, no less liquid than their shadows, offer no angles to the wind. They slip, diminished, neat, through loopholes lesser than themselves.
A. S. J. Tessimond

All cats love a cushioned couch.
Théocrite

Slowly, cautiously, with the careful precautions of a cat lying in wait for prey, she slipped out of the flowerbed, and almost crawling along the wall, she came in front of the balcony.
André Theuriet

In a hieratic pose, the imprint of a goddess.
Josiane Thiriot

One is never sure, watching two cats washing each other, whether it's affection, a taste for it, or a trial run for the jugular.
Helen Thomson

A cat sees no good reason why it should obey another animal, even if it does stand on two legs.
Sarah Thomson

A kitten is so flexible that she is almost double; the hind parts are equivalent to another kitten with which the forepart plays. She does not discover that her tail belongs to her until you tread on it.
Henry David Thoreau

It is not worth while going round the world to count the cats in Zanzibar.
Henry David Thoreau

It often happens that a man is more humanely related to a cat or dog than to any human being.
Henry David Thoreau

The poet is a man who lives at last by watching his moods. An old poet comes at last to watch his moods as narrowly as a cat does a mouse.
Henry David Thoreau

What sort of philosophers are we, who know absolutely nothing about the origin and destiny of cats?
Henry David Thoreau

I prefer dogs to cats and all felines remind me of it at first glance - a sharp and unforgiving glance.
James Thurber

It is said: at night all cats are gray. False: at night, all cats are sleeping.
Patrick Timsit

Poor gentlemen that are forbidden to smoke their cigars because the smoke may wake up the frog or the cat that the lady has in her throat!
Roland Topor

Who loves a cat loves all cats. Who loves his dog does not love the others.

Roland Topor

Two thousand years before our era, the Egyptians had made the conquest of this precious little animal to fight against snakes, but especially against rats and mice that were ravaging grain reserves.

Edward Topsell

The cat carelessly carries the kitten by the scruff of the neck. As a package.

Michel Tournier

Apparently, the cat sees it as a point of honor to be of no use at all, this does not prevent him from claiming a better place at home than the dog.

Michel Tournier

Another cat? Perhaps. For love there is also a season; its seeds must be resown. But a family cat is not replaceable like a wornout coat or a set of tires. Each new kitten becomes its own cat, and none is repeated. I am four cats old, measuring out my life in friends that have succeeded but not replaced one another.

Irving Townsend

Could the purr be anything but contemplative?

Irving Townsend

It was not I who was teaching my cat to gather rosebuds, but she who was teaching me.

Irving Townsend

No one shall deny me my own conclusions, nor my cat her reflective purr.

Irving Townsend

Fear is a slinking cat I find beneath the lilacs of my mind.

Sophie Tunnel

A home without a cat, and a well-fed, well-petted and properly revered cat, may be a perfect home, perhaps; but how can it prove its title?

Mark Twain

A man who carries a cat by the tail learns something he can learn in no other way.

Mark Twain

By what right has the dog come to be regarded as a noble animal? The more brutal and cruel and unjust you are to him the more your fawning and adoring slave he becomes; whereas, if you shamefully misuse a cat

once, she will always maintain a dignified reserve toward you afterward-you will never get her full confidence again.
Mark Twain

Ignorant people think it is the noise which fighting cats make that is so aggravating, but it ain't so; it is the sickening grammar that they use.
Mark Twain

If animals could speak the dog would be a blundering outspoken fellow, but the cat would have the rare grace of never saying a word too many.
Mark Twain

If you shamefully misuse a cat once she will always maintain a dignified reserve toward you afterward. You will never get her full confidence again.
Mark Twain

In an hour I taught a cat and a dog to be friends. I put them in a cage. In another hour I taught them to be friends with a rabbit. In the course of two days I was able to add a fox, a goose, a squirrel and some doves. Finally a monkey. They lived together in peace; even affectionately.
Mark Twain

Of all God's creatures there is only one that cannot be made the slave of the leash; that one is the cat. If man could be crossed with the cat, it would improve man, but it would deteriorate the cat.
Mark Twain

One of the most striking differences between a cat and a lie is that the cat has only nine lives.
Mark Twain

The fence had three coats on it, and Sam had acquired a very big stock of payments - part of a Jew's harp, a brass doorknob, a dead cat, 12 marbles, the handle of a knife and a kitten with one eye.
Mark Twain

The man who sets out to carry a cat by its tail learns something that will always be useful and which never will grow dim or doubtful.
Mark Twain

We should be careful to get out of an experience only the wisdom that is in it and stop there, lest we be like the cat that sits down on a hot stove-lid. She will never sit down on a hot stove-lid again, and that is well; but also she will never sit down on a cold one anymore.
Mark Twain

Commotion for rats at night in the farm where the cat is young.
Sigrid Undset

Cats are smart and aware of it.
Tomi Ungerer

A house without a cat, how empty!
Bertrand Vac

How can one live with a stuffed cat? It is the height of bad taste.
Zoé Valdès

Cats are smarter than dogs. You cannot get eight cats to pull a sled through snow.
Jeff Valdez

Dogs believe they are human. Cats believe they are God.
Jeff Valdez

Is it true cats won't stay in a house when it's haunted?
Jeff Valdez

The motto of the cat: no matter what you did, still try to pretend that it is the fault of the dog.
Jeff Valdez

One hundred cats harvested by villagers. Soaked in gasoline and swung over the fence of the camp with a lit fuse attached to the tail...
You, my friend, I predict that you will one day have very, very big problem with the SPCA.
Jean Van Hamme (Largo Winch)

A cat is never vulgar.
Carl Van Vechten

An ordinary kitten will ask more questions than any five- year -old.
Carl Van Vechten

The cat is the only animal without visible means of support who still manages to earn a living in the city.
Carl Van Vechten

The cat seldom interferes with other people's rights. His intelligence keeps him from doing many of the foolish things that complicate life.
Carl Van Vechten

There is, indeed, no single quality of the cat that man could not emulate to his advantage.
Carl Van Vechten

It was a simple white and gray ball, light as a foam ball, with perfectly round blue eyes.
Fred Vargas

This morning, picking up my cat treasures in the litter, I found in one of them the remains of a 50 euronote.

VDM (Collectif)

Today, my cat peed on the roof of my car. It was dripping all over the ventilation system. Once I start, ventilation starts... and it's a chemical attack.

VDM (Collectif)

Cats are the sentinels of the invisible.

Louis Velle

She played with her pussy
And it was wonderful to see
The white hand and white paw
Frolic in the shadow of the evening.
She hid - the rogue! -
Under these black-threaded mittens
Her murderous nails of agate
Clear and sharp as a razor.
Gave herself airs
Drew in her sharp claws,
But the devil lost nothing...
And in the boudoir, where sonorous
Her laughter tinkled air
Shone four phosphorous points.

Paul Verlaine

I believe cats to be spirits come to earth. A cat, I am sure, could walk on a cloud without going through.

Jules Verne

The poultry dealer's tomcat
A sardine across his shoulder
Embraced by the waist
The cat queen of the cook.

Boris Vian

_ Put your head in my mouth, said the cat, and wait.
_ It may take a long time? asked the mouse.
_ The time someone's treading on my tail, said the cat.

Boris Vian

The smallest feline is a masterpiece.

Léonard de Vinci

As far as I am concerned, I will never be the adoring and imploring slave of a Persian cat, but I like to think that Persian cats consider us all as their servants. They do not lack nerve. It is this nerve that enchants me.
Frédéric Vitoux

The cat is Zen in its essence. Everything else is frivolous.
Frédéric Vitoux

A cat allows you to sleep on the bed. On the edge.
Jenny de Vries

To some blind souls all cats are much alike. To a cat lover every cat from the beginning of time has been utterly and amazingly unique.
Jenny de Vries

You own a dog but you feed a cat.
Jenny de Vries

Intelligence in the cat is underrated.
Louis Wain

The goal of scientists is to build a computer as smart as a cat.
Wamiz

If there was any petting to be done... he chose to do it. Often he would sit looking at me, and then, moved by a delicate affection, come and pull at my coat and sleeve until he could touch my face with his nose, and then go away contented.
Charles Dudley Warner

At Group L, Stoffel oversees six first-rate programmers, a managerial challenge roughly comparable to herding cats.
The Washington Post Magazine

I think one reason we admire cats, those of us who do, is their proficiency in one-upmanship. They always seem to come out on top, no matter what they are doing--or pretend to do. Rarely do you see a cat discomfited. They have no conscience, and they never regret anything. Maybe we secretly envy them.
Barbara Webster

If I called her she would pretend not to hear, but would come a few moments later when it could appear that she had thought of doing so first.
Arthur Weigall

Cats are known to follow their own hidden purposes, did this this make of them, at the best, untrustworthily familiar?
Margaret Weis

_ Why is this kind of a bridge called a cat path? Is it because cats use this a lot?
_ I think it's because they have nine lives.
Margaret Weis & Tracy Hickman

Even when overweight, cats instinctively know the cardinal rule: when fat, arrange yourself in slim poses.
John Weitz

The cat, which is a solitary beast, is single-minded and goes his way alone; but the dog, like his master, is confused in his mind.
H.G. Wells

She feels happy as a cat treading on velvet paws over the heads of humans.
Bernard Werber

Three mice discuss. The first announces: "I can identify spring traps and take the cheese without getting crushed. Just go very fast". "The second answers:" that's nothing. y You know the pink granules of rat poison? Well, I eat them as an appetizer. The third looks at his watch and says with detachment: "Sorry, girls, it is 5 pm, it's time for me to leave you. I have to go and rape the cat. "
Bernard Werber

It is as difficult for a man to understand God as for one atom of cat pancreas to understand a western on human television.
Bernard Werber

There are guide dogs but no guide cats.
Bernard Werber

There are tramp dogs but no tramp cats. When a cat sees that his master can no longer afford to feed him, he abandons him to find another more fortunate. While dogs are what they are but they remain faithful to their master, even if poor, until death.
Bernard Werber

If a dog jumps up into your lap, it is because he is fond of you; but if a cat does the same thing, it is because your lap is warmer.
Alfred North Whitehead

In ancient times cats were worshipped as gods, this they have never forgotten.
Alfred North Whitehead

Recently we were discussing the possibility of making one of our cats Pope, and we decided that the fact she was not Italian and was a female, made the third point, her being a cat, irrelevant.

Katharine Whitehorn

*Bathsheba! to whom no one ever said scat
No worthier cat
Ever sat on a mat,
Or caught a rat.
Requiescat!*

John Whittier

Schrödinger's thought experiment was intended as a discussion of the EPR article, named after its authors - Einstein, Podolsky, and Rosen - in 1935. The EPR article had highlighted the strange nature of quantum superposition. Broadly stated, a quantum superposition is the combination of all the possible states of a system (for example, the possible positions of a subatomic particle). The Copenhagen interpretation implies that the superposition undergoes collapse into a definite state only at the exact moment of quantum measurement.

Schrödinger and Einstein had exchanged letters about Einstein's EPR article, in the course of which Einstein had pointed out that the quantum superposition of an unstable keg of gunpowder will, after a while, contain both exploded and unexploded components.

To further illustrate the putative incompleteness of quantum mechanics, Schrödinger applied quantum mechanics to a living entity that may or may not be conscious. In Schrödinger's original thought experiment, he describes how one could, in principle, transform a superposition inside an atom to a large-scale superposition of a live and dead cat by coupling cat and atom with the help of a "diabolical mechanism". He proposed a scenario with a cat in a sealed box, wherein the cat's life or death was dependent on the state of a subatomic particle. According to Schrödinger, the Copenhagen interpretation implies that the cat remains both alive and dead (to the universe outside the box) until the box is opened.

Schrödinger did not wish to promote the idea of dead-and-alive cats as a serious possibility; quite the reverse, the paradox is a classic reductio ad absurdum. The thought experiment helps to illustrate the bizarreness of quantum mechanics and the mathematics necessary to describe quantum states. Intended as a critique of just the Copenhagen interpretation (the prevailing orthodoxy in 1935), the Schrödinger cat thought experiment remains a topical touchstone for all interpretations of quantum mechanics.

How each interpretation deals with Schrödinger's cat is often used as a way of illustrating and comparing each interpretation's particular features, strengths, and weaknesses
                                                                Wikipedia

A cat doesn't accustom himself well to change if it is someone else's making.
                                                Carole Wilbourn

A cat's behavior is a direct reflection of his feelings.
                                                Carole Wilbourn

The constant challenge of deciphering feline behavior is perhaps one of the most fascinating aspects of owning a cat.
                                                Carole Wilbourn

Lift up your eyes of black satin which are like smooth cushions in which one drowns! Wallow at my feet, you fantastic Sphinx, and recite to me the song of your memories.
                                                Oscar Wilde

Like a graceful vase, a cat, even when motionless, seems to flow.
                                                George F. Will

The phrase domestic cat is an oxymoron.
                                                George F. Will

You can't stop lying, you cat! It must be genetic.
                                                Chris Williams (Bolt)

People who hate cats will be reincarnated as mice.
                                                Jim Willis

The final war will be between Pavlov's dog and Schrödinger's Cat.
                                                Robert Anton Wilson

What is remarkable in cats is that the outer life they reveal to their masters is one of perpetual boredom.
                                                Robley Wilson, Jr.

Women, poets, and especially artists, are like cats delicate natures who can only express their delicacy of feelings
                                                Helen M. Winslow

When mom found my diaphragm, I told her it was a bathing cap for my cat.
                                                Liz Winston

The best you can do is admire the cat's cradle, and maybe knot it up a bit more. History should be a hammock for swinging in and a toy for playing

with, the way cats play. Claw it, chew it, rearrange it and at bedtime it's still a ball of string full of knots. Nobody should mind.
Jeanette Winterson

With his purring and his velvet paw, he became the law of the house.
Francis Witham

As a class, Cats have never completely got over the snootiness caused by that fact that in Ancient Egypt they were worshipped as gods.
P G Wodehouse

You can visualize a hundred cats. Beyond that, you can't. Two hundred, five hundred, it all looks the same.
Jack Wright

If Darwin's theory of evolution was correct, cats would by now be able to operate a can opener.
Larry Wright

All of the people in my building are insane. The guy above me designs synthetic herbals for ceramic cats.
Steven Wright

Curiosity killed the cat, but for a while I was a suspect.
Steven Wright

Why don't they just make mouse-flavored cat food?
Steven Wright

No matter if it is a white cat or a black cat; as long as it can catch mice, it is a good cat.
Deng Xiaoping

Life is like cat vomit; if you do not clean it right away, you'll walk in it.
Xnterna

Brigitte Bardot said: "A cat is a heart with hair around." I shall not venture any comment.
Jean Yanne

Cats are oppressed, dogs terrify them, landladies starve them, boys stone them, everybody speaks of them with contempt. If they were human beings we could talk of their oppressors with a studied violence, add our strength to theirs, even organize the oppressed and like good politicians sell our charity for power.
William Butler Yeats

Minnaloushe creeps through the grass
Alone, important and wise

And lifts to the changing moon
His changing eyes.

William Butler Yeats

I could never understand that kitchen meat did not belong to cats.

Émile Zola

I had a small dog, a griffon of the smallest species, named Fanfan. One day at the Dog Show, in Cours la Reine, I saw him in a cage in the company of a big cat. And he looked at me with eyes so full of tenderness, I told the salesman to release him for a while from that cage. Once on the ground, he began to walk like a dog on wheels. So excited I was that I purchased him.

Emile Zola

I want to tell you that one of the cruellest hours, amid the dreadful hours I've spent, was when I learned the sudden death away from me, of the faithful little companion, who for nine years had never left me.

Emile Zola

It has been said that animals are replacing children for old maids, to whom devotion is not enough. And this is not true, love of animals continues, does not give in to mother love, when it awakes in a woman. This fondness is very special, it is not affected by other feelings, and it does not break them.

Emile Zola

It was his way of caressing, you felt his cold nose and the touch of his sharp teeth, while he danced on his legs, like a baker kneading dough.

Émile Zola

Lawrence looked at the cat's big green eyes, and felt a shudder run over his skin.

Émile Zola

I Love of animals is, like all great sentiments, ridiculous and delicious, full of madness and sweetness, capable of true extravagance as well as of the wisest, strongest will.

Emile Zola

The truth is that everybody loves animals but there are people who do not know that they love them. Can you imagine nature without animals, a prairie without insects, a forest without birds, mountains and plains without living beings? Imagine for a moment man alone and then what an immense desert, what silence, what stillness, what horrible sadness!

Émile Zola

You see, concluded my cat while lying in front of the embers, true happiness, paradise, my dear sir, is to be beaten and locked up in a room where there is meat.

Émile Zola

THE MYSTERY CAT

Poem from Thomas Stearns Eliott
Song from Sarah Brightman

Macavity's a mystery cat, he's called the hidden paw
For he's the master criminal who can defy the law
He's the bafflement of Scotland Yard, the Flying Squad's despair
For when they reach the scene of crime Macavity's not there!

Macavity, Macavity, there's no one like Macavity
He's broken every human law, he breaks the law of gravity
His powers of levitation would make a fakir stare
But when you reach the scene of crime Macavity's not there!
You may seek him in the basement, you may look up in the air
But I tell you once and once again Macavity's not there!

Macavity's a ginger cat, he's very tall and thin
You would know him if you saw him for his eyes are sunken in
His brow is deeply lined with thought, his head is highly domed
His coat is dusty from neglect, his whiskers are uncombed
He sways his head from side to side with movements like a snake
And when you think he's half asleep, he's always wide awake

Macavity, Macavity, there's no one like Macavity
For he's a fiend in feline shape, a monster of depravity
You may meet him in a by-street, you may see him in the square
But when a crime's discovered then Macavity's not there!

He's outwardly respectable, I know he cheats at cards
And his footprints are not found in any files of Scotland Yard's

And when the larder's looted or the jewel case is rifled
Or when the milk is missing or another peke's been stifled
Or the greenhouse glass is broken and the trellis past repair
There's the wonder of the thing Macavity's not there!

Macavity, Macavity, there's no one like Macavity
There never was a cat of such deceitfulness and suavity
He always has an alibi and one or two to spare
What ever time the deed took place Macavity's not there!

And they say that all the cats whose wicked deeds are widely known
I might mention Mungojerrie, I might mention Griddlebone
Are nothing more than agents for the cat who all the time
Just controls the operations: the Napoleon of crime!

Macavity, Macavity, there's no one like Macavity
He's a fiend in feline shape, a monster of depravity
You may meet him in a by-street, you may see him in the square
But when a crime's discovered then Macavity
Macavity, Macavity, Macavity

When a crime's discovered then Macavity's not there!

My dog told me

Anonymous quotations

A cat sees us as dogs... A cat sees himself as a human.
Unknown

A dog has lots of friends because he wags his tail and not his tongue.
Unknown

A dog is worth two policemen.
Unknown

A dog may bark, but his legs will never grow longer.
Unknown

All trees have bark.
All dogs bark.
Therefore, all dogs are trees.
The fallacy of barking up the wrong tree.
Unknown

Amuse the dog with a bone, and the woman with a lie.
Unknown

An incontinent dog is a dog who needs to get out more often than his master wishes.
Unknown

Barking dogs don't bite people they don't know.
Unknown

Customer: Has this dog a good pedigree?
Shop Owner: Has he? Say, if that dog could talk, he wouldn't speak to either of us.
Unknown

Diplomacy is the art of saying 'Nice doggie!'... till you can find a rock.
Unknown

Even a one-eyed dog sleeps with one eye.

Every boy should have two things: a dog, and a mother willing to let him have one

Unknown

Every dog has his day -- but the nights are reserved for the cats.

Unknown

For months he had been her devoted admirer. Now, at long last, he had collected up sufficient courage to ask her the most momentous of all questions.
There are quite a lot of advantages in being a bachelor, he began, but there comes a time when we long for the companionship of another being - a being who will regard one as perfect, as an idol; whom one can treat as one's absolute property; who will be kind and faithful when times are hard; who will share one's joys and sorrows -
To his delight he saw a sympathetic gleam in her eyes. Then she nodded in agreement.
So you're thinking of buying a dog? she said. I think it's a fine idea. Do let me help you choose one!

Unknown

He is your friend, your partner, your defender, your dog. You are his life, his love, his leader. He will be yours, faithful and true, to the last beat of his heart. You owe it to him to be worthy of such devotion.

Unknown

He was a gentleman : his dogs loved him much.

Unknown

I figured we all started out like cats, but then the world put us on a leash and collar and turned us into dogs.

Unknown

I want to be the person my dog thinks I am.

Unknown

If there are no dogs in Heaven, then when I die I want to go where they went.

Unknown

If you wish the dog to follow you, feed him.

Unknown

If your dog doesn't like someone you probably shouldn't either.

Unknown

In a dog-eat-dog world, it is the dogmatic domain of dog lovers to offer dogdom a dog's chance to rise above dog days for a doggone good time.
Unknown

In dog years I'm dead.
Unknown

In the beginning God created man and woman. But seeing them weak, He gave them the dog.
Unknown

It's hard to teach an old dog new tricks.
Unknown

It is no coincidence that the dog cannot talk.
Unknown

Nobody can fully understand the meaning of love until he's owned a dog. He can show you more honest affection with a flick of his tail than a man can gather through a lifetime of handshakes.
Unknown

Of all the people in the world, the best and the worst are drawn to a dead dog. Most turn away. Only the pure of heart can feel its pain. And somewhere in between the rest of us struggle.
Unknown

On the internet, nobody knows you're a dog.
Unknown

One reason a dog is such a lovable creature is his tail wags instead of his tongue.
Unknown

Recipe; a series of step-by-step instructions for preparing ingredients you forgot to buy, in utensils you don't own, to make a dish the dog won't eat.
Unknown

Researchers have discovered that dogs can comprehend a vocabulary of 2,000 words, whereas cats can only comprehend 25 to 50. No one ever asks how many words researchers can comprehend.
Unknown

Should we put a hat on a dog, we could also find a woman for him.
Unknown

Sit, down, stand, stay! Okay, but in return I would love to be petted!
Unknown

Some days you're the dog, other days you're the hydrant.

The cat is mighty dignified until the dog comes by.
Unknown

The cosmonauts became national heroes, but who remembers the monkeys Albert I°, Gordo, Sam, Yorick, Patricia, Mike, Enos and the dogs Dezik, Lisa, Pchelka or Laika?
Yet, without these animals, the space race would not have been as fast and would have caused many human casualties.
Unknown

The dog barks, the cat mews, and the aunt, what does it do?
Unknown

The dog is the only animal that has seen his god.
Unknown

The dog leads the big dog to bite.
Unknown

The dog teaches the child.
Unknown

The dogs bark but the caravan moves on.
Unknown

The more people I meet the more I like my dog.
Unknown

They say that diamonds are a girl's best friend, and a dog is a man's best friend. What does that tell us about which sex is smarter?
Unknown

It is not the pot that the dog licks, it's what's inside.
Unknown

To err is human, to forgive, canine.
Unknown

On tearful woman and limping dog, do not rely.
Unknown

When a dog wags her tail and barks at the same time, how do you know which end to believe?
Unknown

When old dogs bark, it's time to watch out.
Unknown

When you feel dog tired at night, it may be because you've growled all day long.

While the dog pees, the hare escapes.
Unknown

Whoever said let sleeping dogs lie didn't sleep with dogs.
Unknown

Why do dogs still topple trash cans, despite the law that prohibits it?
Unknown

Woman, cat and dog have fleas all along the year.
Unknown

Woman's knee, dog's nose, cat's paw, never have we experienced anything so cold.
Unknown

You do not own a dog, the dog owns you.
Unknown

Read our illustrated quotations in

Pensées Royales Canines
King Barks
Didier Hallépée
Carrefour du Net publisher

bilingual edition

PENSÉES ROYALES CANINES
LES PENSÉES DU KING CHARLES

DIDIER HALLÉPÉE

COLLECTION ARC-EN-CIEL
ANIMAUX

Quotations from authors

When a man's best friend is his dog, that dog has a problem.
Edward Abbey

The dog has one aim in life: to offer his heart.
J.R. Ackerley

It was a particularly stupid dog, so stupid as not to read a teleprompter.
Douglas Adams

When you start to bet on horses, you understand that the dog remains the best friend of man.
Joey Adams

In future years, aircraft will be piloted by a captain and a dog. The working dog will monitor the buttons so the pilot won't touch anything.
Scott Adams

We have never seen a dog intentionally share a bone with another dog.
Smith Adam

When the marmot plays or you caress it, its voice sounds like the murmur of a small dog or the purr of a cat.
Michel Adanson

It is better to be devoured by lions than to be eaten by dogs.
Alex Agase

You courtiers, who cast your disdainful eyes on this Abandoned dog, starving in the streets,
Wait for this rent for fidelity.
Théodore Agrippa d'Aubigné

He is part of my life, it is very stabilizing. But there are also dogs of power, embodying power and domination.
Jean-Jacques Aillagon

Caramel, my King Charles Spaniel, made the cover of a celebrity magazine alongside Obama and Nicolas Sarkozy. I showed him the newspaper. It left him completely indifferent.
Jean-Jacques Aillagon

Whatever we do, this dog's philosophy will be, like the Prince of Orange, often beaten and never defeated.
Jean le Rond d'Alembert

Here we find the moat of thieves. And just as a lizard, with a quick, slick slither, Flicks across the highway from hedge to hedge, Fleeter than a flash, in the battering dog-day weather, A fiery little monster, livid, in a rage, Black as any peppercorn, came and made a dart At the guts of the others, and leaping to engage One of the pair, it pierced him at the part Through which we first draw food; then loosed its grip And fell before him, outstretched and apart.

Dante Alighieri

A dog is loving and faithful, but what's the point of becoming attached to anybody just because he is called your master, beautiful or ugly, funny or boring, good or bad?

Alphonse Allais

As a species, dogs are highly despicable, both for the sickening banality of their affection and for their extraordinary ability to prussianize.

Alphonse Allais

I, who love most animals always professed a passionate dislike for the dog, which I regard as the most abject animal of Creation. The dog is the typically stooge animal, without pride, without dignity, without personality.

Alphonse Allais

If man is truly the king of creation, the dog may, without being accused of exaggeration, be the Baron, at least.

Alphonse Allais

In every dog, there is a beast, though a stupid beast, which, without the excusable need of a personal prey is ready to hurt anyone just to pander to a third person's whim.

Alphonse Allais

The dog is a clown who plays the fool for hours, to have a lump of sugar. He is a coward who would strangle a baby on the slightest sign of his rogue boss.

Alphonse Allais

We are always betrayed by our hounds

Alphonse Allais

We saw dogs being killed in defending their master against a bandit True, but the same dog could be killed by attacking the gentleman on behalf of the bandit, if the bandit had been his master and if the honest man had held the gun that was needed.

Alphonse Allais

Asthma doesn't seem to bother me any more unless I'm in the vicinity of cigars or dogs. The thing that would bother me most would be a dog smoking a cigar.
Steve Allen

The more I know about men the more I like dogs.
Gloria Allred

At the door there was a dog tied, who was keeping watch and was nasty to everyone.
Jacques Amyot

He fed the two dogs so differently that he made one greedy and gluttonous, and the other one good at hunting and retrieving.
Jacques Amyot

He ordered, if a dog bit someone, that the master should be obliged to deliver it attached to a wooden stock: it was a good invention to guard against the dog.
Jacques Amyot

Neither more nor less than dogs of good heart, who never let their prey go nor release their bite until their opponent is crushed.
Jacques Amyot

The hunters cannot stand that their dogs go astray.
Jacques Amyot

These clumps are commonly named dog heads.
Jacques Amyot

They had their bitches and mares covered by the most beautiful dogs and the best stallions they could find.
Jacques Amyot

This dog always followed his master, swimming in the sea alongside his galley, from the shore of firm land, right up to the island of Salamis.
Jacques Amyot

We are easily angered against dogs barking away and kicking donkeys.
Jacques Amyot

Men are like dogs, they bite because they are afraid.
Jean Anouilh

No matter how much I cheat and no matter how hard I shut my eyes there will always be a lost dog somewhere that will prevent me from being happy.
Jean Anouilh

The bachelor lives like a king and dies like a dog, while the married man lives like a dog and dies like a king.
Jean Anouilh

Some see "God" as "dog" spelled backwards. I see "God" as "cat" spelled with a vivid imagination.
Jacob Appel

A huge dog, tied to a chain, was painted on the wall and above it was written in capital letters Beware of the Dog.
Petronius Arbiter

*The Dog and the Cat.
An open foe I much prefer
To a dear friend that scratches.*
Arnadlt

The Academy Awards looks like a competition of elegance for dogs!
Patricia Arquette

With respect to sex, man stands a little above the dog, but he continues to blame the preconceived ideas that prevent him from falling below the dog.
Lucien Arréat

My dog preferably bites diabetic people... He loves sugar.
José Artur

If you can't decide between a Shepherd, a Setter or a Poodle, get them all... adopt a mutt!
ASPCA

Why can't I have a dog myself? But just to kick him! I'm tired of always kicking chickens!
Alexandre Astier

*_ I love dogs.
_ Well then, if you love dogs, why you don't have your own?
_ Because my wife doesn't like them, she prefers cats.
_ You have a cat?
_ No. It's dirty. My wife wants a cat that would not be dirty.
_ A cat, It's less dirty than a dog.
_ What's more dirty, is canaries. My wife didn't want any either, but there I have held out, yes, I did.*
Michel Audiard

At dusk, to dogs and wolves, all cats are grey.
Yvan Audouard

I want to know the music that my dog's tail beats.

Yvan Audouard

They dare to ask me who has a dog, a cat, a turtle, two children, a wife and several mothers, if I like animals!

Yvan Audouard

Two dumb animals, even of different species, are more apt to associate than these two human creatures, and a man would rather be with his dog than with a stranger.

Saint Augustin

As does a horse when he has run, a dog when he has caught the game, a bee when it has made the honey, so a man when he has done a good act does not call out for others to come and see, but he goes on to another act, as a vine goes on to produce again the grapes in season.

Marcus Aurelius

Life is life - whether in a cat, a dog or a man. There is no difference there between a cat or a man. The idea of difference is a human conception - to man's own advantage.

Sri Aurobindo

In a graveyard for dogs we are sure to find only good creatures.

Claude Autant-Lara

I remember that in my early childhood I used to fast, and whenever the fast ended, I would go out taking my meal with me and give it to the stray dogs and cats.

Ahmad Bahgat

Consider the tamed dog, begging for a caress, a glance from his master: is it not the picture of man kneeling before God?

Mikhaïl Bakounine

He's got his dog trained so that it only does it on newspapers. The trouble is it does it when he's reading the blasted things.

Honoré de Balzac

When there is an old maid in a house, guard dogs are useless.

Honoré de Balzac

We speak of love, good and evil... and we cling to these venerable icons as the thirsty tick does to its big warm dog.

Muriel Barbery

A dog, a cat is a heart with hair around.

Brigitte Bardot

I prefer the company of animals to that of humans.

Brigitte Bardot

Should God have wanted to be worshipped, he would have created dogs only. The dog is more apt to love than man is.
René Barjavel

Dogs feel very strongly that they should always go with you in the car, in case the need should arise for them to bark violently at anything right in your ear.
Dave Barry

Dogs have masters, cats have servants.
Dave Barry

You can say any foolish thing to a dog, and the dog will give you this look that says, `My God, you're right! I never would've thought of that!'
Dave Barry

The child is unruly, selfish, devoid of gentleness and patience, and, unlike a pure animal, such as a dog and a cat, he cannot even serve as a confidant to lonely pains.
Charles Baudelaire

Growing up in a farm, I have a small dog, and I had a bike!
Michael Bay

Bernard Tapie and his wife were greatly attached to their dog.
Jean-Michel Baylet

Seeing what qualities are required of a dog, do you know many masters who are worthy of being adopted?
Beaumarchais

A dog bites a man, it's a brief. A man bites a dog, it's a scoop.
Lord Beaverbrook

For fidelity, devotion, love, many a two-legged animal is below the dog and the horse. Happy would it be for thousands of people if they could stand at last before the Judgment Seat and say I have loved as truly and I have lived as decently as my dog.
Henry Ward Beecher

The dog was created especially for children. He is the god of frolicking.
Henry Ward Beecher

Try to go with your dog into a church. St. Francis is not revered everywhere, I guess.
Jo Benchetrit

A boy can learn a lot from a dog: obedience, loyalty, and the importance of turning around three times before lying down.
Robert Charles Benchley

Dachshunds are ideal dogs for small children, as they are already stretched and pulled to such a length that the child cannot do much harm one way or the other.
Robert Charles Benchley

The factory of the future will only have two employees, a man and a dog. The man will be there to feed the dog. The dog will be there to keep the man from tampering with the equipment.
Warren G. Bennis

In the cat's golden eyes and the Setter's deep sweet brown ones, there was all the tenderness of the world.
Juliette Benzoni

My dog is dead, on the other hand. So, if... if I could sleep in your home, you see, just to have a presence, a companion, not to be alone...
Alain Berbérian

It's a fact: President Sarkozy's bitch has been named Clara! The dog's original name was Spirit. The President renamed her Clara when arriving at the Elysee.
Stéphane Bern

Look at the media coverage of Bo at Obama home. Within days, the Portuguese Water Dog has become an international star. Here Obama complies with the tradition of the president's dog and will give the image of a typical American family.
Stéphane Bern

We can better appreciate the importance of royal and presidential dogs when we understand their role as emotional outlet for heads of state condemned to be cautious.
Stéphane Bern

Kings, queens, princes and presidents, women and men can all have a dog.
Perhaps it is because they know that animals, unlike men, never betray.
Stéphane Bern

Qui me amat, amat et canem meum. (Love me, love my dog.)
Saint Bernard

Woman is a wolf to woman.
Tristan Bernard

Dogs are in general two opposite colors, one light and the other darker so that, wherever they are in the house, they can be seen on the furniture with the color of which they would otherwise be confused.

Jacques-Henri Bernardin de Saint-Pierre

Gratitude is a disease of dogs not transmissible to humans.

Antoine Bernheim

A household ceases to be a household when the dog brings the slippers and the woman barks.

Henry Bernstein

Alice is the one who is with me late at night and early in the morning. Alice, who watches over me.

Xavier Bertrand

My dog Alice loves ministerial armchairs, with a preference for the large garden of the Department of Labour.

Xavier Bertrand

We can love dogs without becoming President of the Republic. Who loves dogs loves humans.

Xavier Bertrand

Am I a dog, that thou comest to me with staves?

Bible

As a dog returneth to his vomit, so a fool returneth to his folly.

Bible

Do not give what is holy to dogs, and do not throw your pearls before swine, or they will trample them under their feet, and turn and tear you to pieces.

Bible

Like one who seizes a dog by the ears is a passer-by who meddles in a quarrel not his own.

Bible

To all the living there is hope for a living dog is better than a dead lion.

Bible

Yet dogs eat some of the crumbs which fall from their masters' table.

Bible

All these people, politicians, thieves, careerist officials have exploited France systematically. They believe that everything is going well and they feel, vis-à-vis the unfortunate citizen whose foot struck their bowl, the fierce anger of the dog from whom you want to snatch a bone.

Jean-Baptiste Bidegain

Cerberus, n. The watch-dog of Hades, whose duty it was to guard the entrance - against whom or what does not clearly appear; everybody, sooner or later, had to go in there, and nobody wanted to carry off the gates.

Ambrose Bierce

Dog, n. A subsidiary Deity designed to catch the overflow and surplus of the world's worship.... His master works for the means wherewith to purchase the idle wag of the Solomonic tail, seasoned with a look of tolerant recognition.

Ambrose Bierce

Effect, n. The second of two phenomena which always occur together in the same order. The first, called a Cause, is said to generate the other - which is no more sensible than it would be to declare the rabbit the cause of a dog who pursues it.

Ambrose Bierce

J, n. A consonant in English, but some nations use it as a vowel... from a Latin verb, jacere, to throw, because when a stone is thrown at a dog, the dog's tail assumes that shape.

Ambrose Bierce

Medicine, n. A stone flung down the Bowery to kill a dog in Broadway.

Ambrose Bierce

Physician, n. One upon whom we set our hopes when ill and our dogs when well.

Ambrose Bierce

Reverence, n. The spiritual attitude of a man to a god and a dog to a man.

Ambrose Bierce

Zeus, n. The chief of Grecian gods, adored by the Romans as Jupiter and by the modern Americans as God, Gold, Mob and Dog.

Ambrose Bierce

A dog is the only thing on earth that loves you more than he loves himself.

Josh Billings

Don't mistake pleasure for happiness. They are a different breed of dogs.

Josh Billings

Money will buy you a pretty good dog, but it won't buy the wag of his tail.

Josh Billings

Newfoundland dogs are good at saving children from drowning, but you must have a pond of water handy and a child, or else there will be no profit in having a Newfoundland at home.

Josh Billings

Returning from a walk with his dog in this so typically British rain, his lordship will enter carefree.
Binet (les Bidochons)

The little King Charles – so human – is the true aristocrat of the dog world.
M. Joyce Birchall

Keep your eye on the main chance and don't stop to kick every barking dog.
Morton C. Blackwell

A dog starving at his master's gate foreshadows the ruin of the state.
William Blake

What is the use for a man to conquer the world if he can't prevent his dog from shitting on the floor.
Claude Blanchard

Things that upset a terrier may pass virtually unnoticed by a Great Dane.
Smiley Blanton

You gonna bark all day, little doggy, or are you gonna bite?
Mr. Blonde

A dog will make eye contact. A cat will, too, but a cat's eyes don't even look entirely warm-blooded to me, whereas a dog's eyes look human though less controlled. A dog will look at you as if to say, "What do you want me to do for you? I'll do anything for you." Whether a dog can, in fact, do anything for you if you don't have sheep (I never have) is another matter. The dog is willing to help.
Roy Blount Jr.

I do not know what the cat may have eaten. Usually I know exactly what the cat has eaten. Not only have I fed it to the cat, at the cat's insistence, but the cat has thrown it up on the rug, and someone has tracked it on to the other rug. I do not know why cats are such habitual vomiters. They do not seem to enjoy it, judging by the sounds they make while doing it. It's their nature. A dog is going to bark. A cat is going to vomit.
Roy Blount Jr.

A blind man once told me that his dog cost him "the eyes of the head".
Léon Bloy

It's time to pay your term, or go and die in the street, among the children of dogs!
Léon Bloy

The perfect stupidity of this sensualist always with an erection can also be observed in the eyes of a bewildered cow or of a peeing dog.

Léon Bloy

Dogs come when they're called. Cats take a message and call you back.
Mary Bly

Apart from the Saints and a few stray dogs, we are all more or less contaminated by the disease of sadness.
Christian Bobin

A Mouse is afraid of a cat, a cat is afraid of a dog.
Christian Bobin

What is the name of the dog that bites its master? Glory.
Christian Bobin

He loved women as much as a dog loves being beaten with a stick.
Boccace

Ah! It's a dog?
Dany Boon

If you do not like dogs, you do not like loyalty, you do not like faithfulness towards you, so you are not faithful.
Napoléon Bonaparte

Youth will be served, every dog has his day, and mine has been a fine one.
George Borrow

It was a great upland dog, with long hair, tough fangs and a resolute fighting spirit which was reassuring.
Henri Bosco

Man is a wolf to man, which you will agree, is not very nice for the wolf.
Serge Bouchard

Ah! Fake animal lovers who start patting a pretty woman's dog with the hope of finding their way to her heart in the hair of the animal!
Philippe Bouvard

Animals were created by God to give men a sense of superiority.
Philippe Bouvard

Dogs being banned from paradise seems to prove that loyalty is not considered a cardinal virtue.
Philippe Bouvard

I've often been disappointed by men. Sometimes by women. Rarely by work. Never by dogs.
Philippe Bouvard

My dog totally ignores metaphysical anguish, VAT, Andre Comte-Spongieux and lifelong learning, enjoys a peaceful life and benefits without asking useless questions from everything life has to offer: a ray of sunshine, a piece of chop, a piece of sugar, the butcher's bitch.
Philippe Bouvard

If loyalty did not exist to tie them up, it would now be very difficult to distinguish a man from a dog: they both hide their features under their hair.
Philippe Bouvard

The streets are full of obsessed people, schizophrenics and paranoids who walk their tics and obsessions as others walk their dog.
Philippe Bouvard

Life which comes
And goes
Leaves us speechless
Like dogs...
Jacques Brel

To get a Beagle is saying goodbye to pills for nerves.
Félix Breton

In prehistoric times, the dog becomes the companion of man. It helps to hunt, guards his house and breeding cattle.
Alyse Brisson

For it is the mutt o'the barrier
the for'paws, what! Dogs of Paris...
Those who will not be impounded.
Aristide Bruant

In order to keep a true perspective of one's importance, everyone should have a dog that will worship him and a cat that will ignore him.
Dereke Bruce

My dog can't slow down in the entrance, it's all marble.
Carla Bruni-Sarkozi

My son Aurelian has a Chihuahua named Tumi. Alas, it doesn't get along well with Lili, my cat. I fear the worst with Estrie, a Labrador dog that Bernard Laporte has brought us from Quebec!
Carla Bruni-Sarkozi

What's good with dogs is that they live for only ten years on average. You end up burying them, it gives us the impression of being eternal.
Serge Brussolo

The dog is the only animal whose loyalty is put to the test, the only one who understands his name and knows his masters' voice.
Georges Louis Leclerc, comte de Buffon

Dogs have all the inner qualities that may attract the attention of man.
Georges Louis Leclerc, comte de Buffon

I'd rather have an inch of a dog than miles of a pedigree.
Dana Burnet

Does the moon care if the dog barks?
Robert Burton

Like dogs in a wheel, birds in a cage, or squirrels in a chain, ambitious men still climb and climb, with great labor, and incessant anxiety, but never reach the top.
Robert Burton

Like a hog, or dog in the manger, he doth only keep it because it shall do nobody else good, hurting himself and others.
Robert Burton

Study hard, and you might grow up to be President. But let's face it: Even then, you'll never make as much money as your dog.
George H.W. Bush

The Way of the Samurai is found in death.
When it comes to either/or, there is only the quick choice of death.
It is not particularly difficult.
Be determined and advance.
To say that dying without reaching one's aim is to die a dog's death is the frivolous way of sophisticates.
When pressed with the choice of life or death, it is not necessary to attain one's aim.
We all want to live.
And in a large part our logic is fashioned by what we like.
But not having attained our aim and continuing to live is cowardice.
This is a thin dangerous line.
To die without attaining one's aim IS a dog's death and fanaticism.
But there is no shame in this.
This is the substance of the Way of the Samurai.
If by setting one's heart right every morning and evening,
One is able to live as though one's body were already dead,
He gains freedom in the Way
His whole life will be blameless,
And he will succeed in his calling.

Bushido

The great pleasure of a dog is that you may make a fool of yourself with him and not only will he not scold you, but he will make a fool of himself too.
Samuel Butler

A dog wags its tail with its heart
Martin Buxbaum

All men are congenitally villains. And I only regret that, not being a dog, I cannot bite them.
Lord Byron

Here rest the remains of one who possessed beauty without vanity, strength without insolence, courage without ferocity, and all the virtues of man without his vices. This praise, which is only a flat and meaningless flattery if addressing human ashes, is but a just tribute to the memory of Boatswain, a dog born in Newfoundland in May 1803, who died in Newstead-Abbey, Nov. 18, 1808.
Lord Byron

The poor dog, in life the firmest friend,
The first to welcome, the foremost to defend.
Lord Byron

Personally, I would not give a fig for any man's religion from which neither horse nor cat nor dog drew any benefits. Life in any form is our perpetual responsibility.
S. Parkes Cadman

She had a swan's neck, a cat's eyes, an eagle's gaze, a wasp's waist, a gazelle's legs, a lion's temperament, a dog's character. Yet she was a woman.
Louis Calaferte

The thief knows a thief and the wolf a wolf.
Callimaque

So for relics: everything is so jumbled and confused, we should not worship the bones of a martyr without being in danger of worshipping the bones of a robber or thief, or of a donkey or a dog or a horse.
Jean Calvin

On the green banks of Shannon, when Sheelah was nigh,
No blithe Irish lad was so happy as I,
No harp like my own could so cheerily play,
And wherever I went was my poor dog Tray.

Thomas Campbell

I told him that the pound kept dogs three days at the disposal of their owners and then they did whatever they liked.

Albert Camus

My life is nothing. What matters are the reasons of my life. I am not a dog.

Albert Camus

With dogs and people, it's love in big splashy colors. When you're involved with a cat, you're dealing in pastels.

Louis Camuti

Matignon, his "dog-like job" and his leash.

Le Canard Enchaîné

I'm a mog. Half man, half dog. I'm my own best friend

John Candy

A dog is a pet another dog instinctively recognizes as such.

Elias Canetti

If dogs could talk, perhaps we should find it as hard to get on with them as we do with people.

Karel Capek

All dogs, when they are in trouble, start to yawn.

Truman Capote

Dogs are not our whole life, but they make our lives whole.

Roger Caras

Dogs have given us absolutely all they have. We are the center of their universe. We are the focus of their love and faith and trust. They serve us in return for scraps. It is without a doubt the best deal man has ever made.

Roger Caras

The dog growls when it's angry and wags its tail when happy. Me, I growl when I'm pleased and wag my tail when am angry. So I'm mad! (Cheshire cat).

Lewis Carroll

They had three men dressed up as three devils, who were clad in skins of dogs, black and white, and had horns as long as their arms and whose faces were painted coal-black.

Jacques Cartier

Man is the dog's best friend.

Paul Carvel

Diplomacy is the art of saying Oh, the pretty dog while looking round for a stick.
Wynn Catlin

The dog loves passionately foul odours. If the dog is loyal to man, it's because man stinks.
François Cavanna

My dog is an atheist: he no longer believes in me.
François Cavanna

When we stutterers speak of the devil between us, we never see the tail of him.
François Cavanna

The leaders of peoples see themselves as shepherds, they are often no more than herding dogs.
Gilbert Cesbron

Bourgeois cannot stand being classified by philosophers. That means being questioned, laid bare, killed, forced to spit what they hide: as aggressive as dogs, behind good-natured attitudes.
Vincent Cespedes

The nobility, noblemen say, is an intermediary between the king and the people... Yes, just as the hunting dog is an intermediary between the hunter and the hare.
Chamfort

Flatterers look like friends the way wolves look like dogs.
George Chapman

An animal never regains the love she gives you.
Madeleine Chapsal

The dog represents all that is best in man.
Etienne Charlet

To tell the truth, what is best in man is the dog.
Nicolas Charlet

Practice recalling your anger like a shepherd calling his dog.
Emile-Auguste Chartier (Alain)

Thou therefore who want to know, first be an astronomer. And as much as you can, all things consider astronomically, so the old sense of the word consider, yes, astronomically, these men, that war and that peace, and even your dog...
Emile-Auguste Chartier (Alain)

Horses jumped, pranced, reared up amid the crowd like dogs caressing their masters.
François René, vicomte de Chateaubriand

There are degrees among the poor as there are among the rich; it can go from the man who covers himself with his dog in winter, to the one who shivers in his tattered rags.
François René, vicomte de Chateaubriand

When the Dutch suffer a gale at sea, they retreat into the interior of the ship, close the hatches and drink punch, leaving a dog on the bridge to bark at the storm.
François René, vicomte de Chateaubriand

Even if it happens that some people behave like beasts, dogs continue to remain beasts.
Noëlle Châtelet

Thank goodness there are different kinds of dogs.
Louis Chevalier

Two qualities are required of a spokesperson. It is that "it speaks", to use Lacan's phrase, and, like the bitch of Malebranche, that it does not think.
Julien Cheverny

This little dog is very smart!
Jacques Chirac

The ups and downs of life affect everyone, even a small dog that had everything to be happy.
Bernadette Chirac

I was reading in a room, Sumo was lying on the floor. My husband arrived, and he jumped at him! He can jump very high, can a Bichon. He was bitten in the stomach. I was very scared because there was blood. It's terrible, small teeth like that. And he was wild! He tried to jump again and bite.
Bernadette Chirac

A dog is a reasoning animal. He is intelligent; he makes his deductions from his own point of view. There are people who can enter a house and others who cannot - that a dog does not take long to learn. Well, who is all the time trying to get in, knocking at the door two or three times a day - and is never invited to come in? The postman. So he is someone clearly undesirable for the householder. He is dismissed every time and yet he keeps coming back and trying his luck! So the duty of the dog is clear - it should help drive the intruder away and bite him if possible. This is the most logical approach.

Agatha Christie

A master is often kind to his dog. He goes into the garden and throws a ball to the gentle beast. A dog may also show kindness to his master. He kills a rabbit or a rat and just drops it off at his feet. Then he wags his tail.

Agatha Christie

According to legend, Pekes, originally, used to be lions. And they still have the heart of a lion.

Agatha Christie

Ah, what scent, what heady scent! There is a charming little female around. Yes... yes I would give anything to meet her.

Agatha Christie

An intelligent dog, no doubt. Smarter than the police.

Agatha Christie

Dogs, I ask you! All the time throwing up and doing their dirt everywhere!

Agatha Christie

Dogs are wise. They crawl into a quiet corner to lick their wounds and only return to the world once back on their feet.

Agatha Christie

Having barked with all the ferocity he considered essential for a good guard dog, he understood rightly that nobody had come to steal the spoons or attack his masters.

Agatha Christie

He turned his head towards her and stood rubbing his nose against her calf.

Agatha Christie

He was a nasty brat and a brute! He kept torturing cats and strays and bullying his classmates.

Agatha Christie

He was ready to bark and bite at the same time, if deemed necessary.

Agatha Christie

I am a good guard dog, ain't I? But do not worry. It's just for fun. It is also my role, of course. It is necessary that I let it be known that there is a dog in this house! How boring this morning! It's a blessing to have something to do now. You're coming to see us? I hope so. How boring it is, you know! I would like to have a bit of a chat.

Agatha Christie

I was the cat watching the mouse, the dog smelling his scent without ever losing it. And the squirrel too. Now, I'll look in my reserve for some nuts I put aside long ago.
Agatha Christie

I'll slaughter you! he growled. Cut you to shreds. That'll teach you to try to enter this house! Wait a little and just taste my teeth!
Agatha Christie

It's amazing, just imagine, what dogs can know.
Agatha Christie

It's like dogs: they smell death. Then they toss their heads back and howl.
Agatha Christie

Let me see... You've recently talked to a Spaniel, my little finger tells me. The dogs here are idiots, if you ask me. What's that? A cat? That is interesting! Too bad he is not here. He would have provided a nice hunt. Hmm... Not bad, this bull terrier.
Agatha Christie

Man loves and respects his dog. He indulges his whims, he praises his intelligence and wisdom to his friends. But just imagine that the relationship may well be reversed! The dog loves his master, he indulges his whims, he also praises his qualities, his sagacity, his intelligence. And just as a man who does not want to shakes his laziness off because his dog loves to go for a walk, so the dog shall try to give his master what the latter wants most in the world.
Agatha Christie

Men are not little boys that we must defend and protect. They have to face tigers, faithful Spaniels, creatures enamored of the style "yours 'till death", shrews, nags, streaks... And that's not the half of it!
Agatha Christie

Nice to see you, I assure you, he remarked, sniffing our ankles. My apologies for the noise, but I 'm doing my job, ain't I? I must be careful who we let in, you know. But it's a boring life and I am very happy to have visitors. I wonder if you have a dog, have you?
Agatha Christie

Okay, that's what you are made for, my dear slave. We'll go out and walk in the street. Surrounded by a thousand odours, hopefully.
Agatha Christie

People are despicable. They are like dogs. However deep we may bury what we want at all costs to get rid of, a dog will always unearth it.
Agatha Christie

She had the air of an abandoned dog. And now she wore that expression of incredulous delight of the dog that, for the sake of peace and quiet, you decide will have a walk with you.
Agatha Christie

She looked like a fox terrier facing a rat hole.
Agatha Christie

The dog licked her face, ears and neck and wagged frantically its tail.
Agatha Christie

The job of dogs is not thinking. Their place is in the yard to scare the burglars away.
Agatha Christie

They use guinea pigs, I think... It is cruel... but less than dogs, of course... or even cats.
Agatha Christie

What if we discover that we both love dogs and cats and that we hate red, this is what is called a "common thread" between us?
Agatha Christie

When archaeologists begin to dig, they dig like crazy and are no longer able to stop! A bit like Fox-Terriers.
Agatha Christie

Whenever you need me to defend you, my good master, I'll be there, less than a step away.
Agatha Christie

While it is sometimes difficult to put a dog on the run, it is still more difficult to make him give it up once he has smelled an odour.
Agatha Christie

Who's there? We would swear that some maniac has brought a Spaniel who is exhausted from running after a rabbit.
Agatha Christie

You've never seen a trapped dog? It bares its teeth at anyone who tries to touch it.
Agatha Christie

You're chaining me up, aren't you? Obviously, I know it's pretty flattering. This proves that I I'm a valuable dog.
Agatha Christie

You could read, deep in his faded blue eyes, a little silent supplication, that of the dog hoping against hope that his master will take him for a ride.
Agatha Christie

How dreadful are the curses which Mohammedanism lays on its votaries! Besides the fanatical frenzy, which is as dangerous in a man as hydrophobia in a dog, there is this fearful fatalistic apathy.
Winston Churchill

All dogs look up to you. All cats look down on you. Only the pig looks at you as an equal.
Winston Churchill

Our dog chases people on a bike. We've had to take it from him.
Winston Churchill

The Bulldog's nose has been slanted backwards so that he can breathe without letting himself go.
Winston Churchill

That's what sheep are like. They obey the dogs that obey the shepherds who follow the stars.
Charles-Albert Cingria

If the dog is the most despised of animals it is because man knows himself too well to be able to enjoy a companion that is so faithful.
Emil Michel Cioran

Even the stupidest cat seems to know more than any dog.
Eleanor Clark

The fault of the dog is to be an animal both dirty and affectionate.
Paul Claudel

What a sad fate for a dog that belongs to no one!
Paul Claudel

I used to look at my dog Smokey and think, 'If you were a little smarter you could tell me what you were thinking,' and he'd look at me like he was saying, 'If you were a little smarter, I wouldn't have to.'
Fred Jung Claus

The time comes to every dog when it ceases to care for people merely for the sake of biscuits or bones, or even of caresses, and walks out. When a dog really loves, it prefers the person who gives it nothing, and perhaps is too ill ever to take it out for exercise, to all the liberal cooks and active dog-boys in the world.
Frances P. Cobbe

If I prefer cats to dogs, it is because there is no police cat.
Jean Cocteau

Poetry is a religion without hope. The poet wears himself out knowing that the masterpiece is, after all, like the act of a clever performing dog on a shaky ground.

Jean Cocteau

The masterpiece is after all the act of a clever performing dog on a shaky ground.

Jean Cocteau

You say you love flowers and you cut their tails, you say you love dogs and you put them on a leash, you say you love birds and you put them in cages, you say you love me, then I'm afraid.

Jean Cocteau

A dog that I myself trained as a watchdog that must bark as soon as he hears a bell.

Sidonie Gabrielle Claudine Colette

Bulldogs are adorable, with faces like toads that have been sat on.

Sidonie Gabrielle Claudine Colette

She was entrusted with kittens to lick, puppies of foreign hounds.

Sidonie Gabrielle Claudine Colette

Yes, in my life, there were lots of dogs but there was the cat.

Sidonie Gabrielle Claudine Colette

He never answered to the names we chose for him. So we called him The Dog.

Colombo

This dog may not be the most beautiful dog in the world, by far, but I can tell you that if there was a contest for the cutest dog, then he would have his kennel covered with medals because, as regards love, sir, this dog is a true champion. It is love made dog.

Colombo

An Arab accused of bribing an official! He had given a lump of sugar to a police dog!

Coluche

Sometimes, we have more contacts with a poor dog than with a rich man.

Coluche

There are people who have children just because they cannot afford a dog.

Coluche

We must treat the outside as the inside. The skin of a tiger or a leopard does not look different from the skin of a dog or a sheep, if the hair is scraped.
Confucius

I do not like animals
They are full of fleas
And are smelly
However often you give them orders
They do as they please.
François Coppée

I never married because I have three pets at home that answer the same purpose as a husband. I have a dog that growls every morning, a parrot that swears all afternoon, and a cat that comes home late at night
Marie Corelli

Besides, let the venerers, following their track, abstain from running down the deer, if it rests; let them acquaint the huntsmen and press the deer gently, without letting the dogs go at it until I give command.

Bind the rascal up; the leash of your dogs
Can be used for lack of other bonds.
Pierre Corneille

One dog moaned and the head of the garrison stroked her head.
Bernard Cornwell

The dogs barked and the tocsin was sounded. But no French assaulted the breach. Instead, when the mist rose over the river, the besiegers catapulted the corpses of animals into the city. The dogs had been gutted and butchered to warn the garrison of the fate that lay in store for them.
Bernard Cornwell

The dog had promised never to bite
And the cat swore never to scratch
And since that day, they have obeyed the order
And the dog and cat are friends forever.
Michèle Corti

My greatest accomplishment in life (other than two awesome sons)? I have never met a dog who didn't like me.
Bewick Cory

Unable to be, to my great regret, the lucky trucker dog who, on top of the parcels, sheltered from retaliations, barks at the company, meaning how little it makes of it...

Georges Courteline

Mad dogs and Englishmen go out in the midday sun; The Japanese don't care to, the Chinese wouldn't dare to; Hindus and Argentines sleep soundly from twelve to one, But Englishmen detest the afternoon nap.
Noel Coward

When a dog bites a man, that is no news, but when a man bites a dog, that is news.
Charles Anderson Dana

I suspect death to be infinitely more faithful than a dog, a toothbrush or a woman.
Michel Dansel

Nothing is more unpleasant in our miserable lives than the occasional impression of having missed something...
Except, of course, when that something is a dog turd...
Dany

A dog in a hurry always remembers that the straight line is the shortest path from a fist to a bone.
Frédéric Dard

If you want your dog's puppies to be treated well, do not give them, sell them.
Frédéric Dard

When their stomachs are crammed full, they get up, whistle the dogs, load the guns, and go on the hunt.
Alphonse Daudet

Chance is more docile than we think. We must love it. And as soon as we do, there is an end of chance, that unexpected big dog in a sleepy game of skittles
René Daumal

The dog is a yes-animal. Very popular with people who can't afford a yes-man.
Robertson Davies

A strange dog that follows you is a sign of luck. If howling, it is a sign of bad luck.
Jim Davis (Garfield)

Ah, the great rivalry between cats and dogs!
Jim Davis (Garfield)

Dogs, how not to love them?
Jim Davis (Garfield)

Dogs, you cannot live with them, you cannot live without them.
                                    Jim Davis (Garfield)

Dogs are far too busy to do nothing.
                                    Jim Davis (Garfield)

Dogs cool themselves by pulling their tongue.
                                    Jim Davis (Garfield)

Dogs look busy, even when they do nothing.
                                    Jim Davis (Garfield)

Dogs understand nothing about wool balls.
                                    Jim Davis (Garfield)

Dogs do not vote.
                                    Jim Davis (Garfield)

He hunted his tail so much that it ended up hiding.
                                    Jim Davis (Garfield)

I have been a dog for only two minutes and I already hate cats.
                                    Jim Davis (Garfield)

I love this dog.
                                    Jim Davis (Garfield)

I wonder how dogs can remember where they buried their bones.
                                    Jim Davis (Garfield)

If I am to believe your personal card, I have to bark at you, right?
                                    Jim Davis (Garfield)

If you throw a ball to a dog, he will make a dart at it. But this is not the case of a cat / this is not what a cat will do. (variante)
                                    Jim Davis (Garfield)

It is not wise to bite the hand that feeds you.
                                    Jim Davis (Garfield)

Leashes are the next best thing after bread and butter.
                                    Jim Davis (Garfield)

Maybe Charlie Brown needs a cat?
                                    Jim Davis (Garfield)

My faithful dog, always so cheerful, always so cuddly!
                                    Jim Davis (Garfield)

People who have pets live longer.
                                    Jim Davis (Garfield)

Pets have their fifteen minutes of madness.

Jim Davis (Garfield)

The Chihuahua said: "I try to make myself very small."
Jim Davis (Garfield)

The dog cannot bear change.
Jim Davis (Garfield)

The flea goes on holiday. She takes a greyhound for the Côte d'Azur.
Jim Davis (Garfield)

The problem with dogs: there is no button to turn them off.
Jim Davis (Garfield)

We feel safer with a dog at home.
Jim Davis (Garfield)

What a horrible nightmare, I dreamed I was a dog!
Jim Davis (Garfield)

What do we get if we remove half the brain of a cat? An intelligent dog! Author's note: do not compare dog and cat to man and woman...
Jim Davis (Garfield)

What is special about the friendship between animals and their masters? Each of us may need to be loved?
Jim Davis (Garfield)

What would life be like if it was cats and dogs who were in charge?
Jim Davis (Garfield)

Why do dogs hunt their tails?
Jim Davis (Garfield)

You are always in my legs, thank you.
Jim Davis (Garfield)

You have decided to have animals who love you : you're not a failure.
Jim Davis (Garfield)

Dogs have more love than integrity. They've been true to us, yes, but they haven't been true to themselves.
Clarence Day

Seeing some of the monuments against which they defecate, you would think that dogs are pure aesthetes.
Jean Delacour

Animals attack animals to eat. Not for fun!
Alain Delon

Dogs are like men, with fewer defects.

Alain Delon

Dogs show absolute loyalty and love for their master, be it a bum, President Mitterrand or Alain Delon. It's beautiful.
Alain Delon

According to me, he who causes suffering to an animal is worse than a beast. He is the animal.
Alain Delon

The day when we're gone, there will still be animals. They will have a quieter life than with us around.
Alain Delon

Who tortures a dog can torture a man.
Alain Delon

When choosing a pet, remember that a dog will consider you as his family, and a cat as a domestic.
Ron Dentinger

All the things we get dogs, horses and monkeys to do are only movements of fear, hope or joy, so they can do them without any thought.
René Descartes

Whoever hates his dog will have it that he is mad.
Eustache Deschamps

I never noticed that there was that much difference between dogs and cats!
Desperate Housewives

_ She has some excuses: her mother is in jail, her father is gone...
_ Yes, and if her dog was dead, that would be enough to write a song!
Desperate Housewives

I prefer the eye of a dog when he beats his tail, to the tail of Le Pen when he bats an eye.
Pierre Desproges

I hate you, I hate all humanity. The more I know men, the more I love my dog. The more I know women, the less I love my bitch.
Pierre Desproges

My job was also, on the other hand, before school time, to walk out the watchdogs of the store for a pee.
Louis-Ferdinand Destouches (Céline)

Let the dog take seriously the bone that has withstood the hyena.
Massa Makan Diabaté

After all, rats also had the right to live, just as a human being has. But, of course, the dog could not understand it; killing was an instinct firmly rooted in the animal.
Philip K. Dick

The cats, joined by a small dog, came and walked under his feet, preventing him from moving as he tried to leave the hut.
Philip K. Dick

Let sleeping dogs lie.
Charles Dickens

Weak men are the dogs of strong men.
Denis Diderot

I am called a dog because I fawn on those who give me anything, I yelp at those who refuse, and I stick my teeth into rascals.
Diogène

Being a celebrity doesn't even seem to keep the fleas off our dogs - and if being a celebrity won't give me an advantage over a couple of fleas, then I guess there can't be much in being a celebrity after all.
Walt Disney

Get a good idea and stay with it. Dog it and work at it until it's the right one.
Walt Disney

If you want to keep your marrowbone, you'd better learn to love cats.
Walt Disney

The dog has an instinct for hunting. That's why I hunt.
Walt Disney

Life after the elections, 1997: Elizabeth's back at the Red Cross, and I walk the dog.
Bob Dole

The man who has just made a joke and then has to explain it is like a hunter who did not have a dog and would be obliged to pick his game up himself.
Maurice Donnay

This eased the tense atmosphere: one of the unionists adored dogs.
Renaud Donnedieu de Vabres

Whenever I had an official meeting or negotiations, my dog Diego was exfiltrated.
Renaud Donnedieu de Vabres

If only men could love each other like dogs do, the world would be a paradise.
James Douglas

A dog, a huge dog, horrible, coming out of Hell... A foul beast, a giant dog with sparkling eyes and glowing hair.
Sir Arthur Conan Doyle

The curious incident of the dog in the nighttime. The dog did nothing in the nighttime. That was the curious incident, remarked Sherlock Holmes.
Sir Arthur Conan Doyle

This dog understood much of our language.
Michel Drucker

I hope that my dog Olga is somewhere and I will find her again one day.
Michel Drucker

I love this bitch! This is the sweetest and most tender animal I have ever had!
Michel Drucker

Suddenly she heard some exclamations, and, on her left, the horns sounding to let the hounds loose, and the venerers' voices egging on the hounds.
Maurice Druon

The dog wears a bell with a light sound. Gentle enough to avoid alerting the bird too early.
Joseph Dubosc

As for his employees, servants--and they are many-- he treats them like dogs and always discourages them.
Georges Duhamel

His agitation was so great she placed the cat food under the dog's nose and the dog's soup under the cat's nose.
Alexandre Dumas

Seeing the dog so happy, watching with eyes so intelligent, talking with accents so nuanced, the doctor's idea grew stronger than ever of making the dog he had saved the smart intermediary, the active link between the human will and the nothingness of the poor idiotic girl it was his task to help to live.
Alexandre Dumas

Dogs are in vogue today. The Lord of Hounds has precedence over me.
Alexandre Dumas

Silence is the best friend of man, even more so than the dog...
Françoise Dumoulin-Tessier

Rambunctious, rumbustious, delinquent dogs become angelic when sitting.
Dr. Ian Dunbar

In his whole life, John Wayne may well kill as many as six thousand Indians, never will he shoot down a dog or hurt a child; that's what you call a career.
Jacques Dutronc

TV is as faithful a companion as a dog but less messy, unless we light it too often. It's a wood fire of sorts.
Jacques Dutronc

Dogs laugh, but they laugh with their tails. What puts man in a higher state of evolution is that he has got his laugh on the right end.
Max Eastman

In the beginning, God created man, but seeing him so feeble, He gave him the dog.
Warren Eckstein

When he visited the king, Gorges Clemenceau asked the king if, on his return to England, he would put his dog in quarantine for law enforcement. "Certainly not," replied the king, "I make the rules, can't I break them?"
Edouard VII

Cats don't bark—and consumers today don't salivate on command as they seemed to a couple of decades ago. Consumers today behave more like cats than Pavlov's pooch. Times have changed—and so must we.
Bryan Eisenberg

What counts is not necessarily the size of the dog in the fight - it's the size of the fight in the dog.
Dwight Eisenhower

Again I must remind you that a dog's a dog - a cat's a cat.
Thomas Stearns Eliott

Dogs are like men, you can con them by playing on their feelings.
James Ellroy

Dogs walked with their tails between their legs. They groaned. They were scared to death
James Ellroy

I do not share his need to be loved by the destitute. I have a pet dog that fills my need for spontaneous affection.
James Ellroy

_ I have two Airedales.
_ They are good dogs. They get along well with children.
James Ellroy

I would like spending my days sitting here, talking to the dog.
James Ellroy

The bartender yawned. Stray dogs were slouching about the room.
James Ellroy

In life it's better to be rich and healthy than as poor and sick as a dog!
Gad Elmaleh

Master varlet you are wrong, I say,
let the dog that sleeps lie.
Jehan Erars

Dog: Animal able to speak when necessary, as evidenced by this German shepherd who, exasperated by his master, who asked him for the fortieth consecutive time to bring back the baball in its moumouth, told him to go fufuck himself!
Escayrol

Panzer Dog: German shepherd trained for armored fighting in the African jungle.
Escayrol

Then the winged dog of Zeus, the tawny eagle, will voraciously tear into pieces large chunks of your body... he'll feast to the end on the black pasture of your liver.
Eschyle

I implore the gods for some respite from the weary task of this long year's watch that, lying on the Atridae's roof on my bended arm, dog- like, I have kept, marking the course of all the night stars, those potentates blazing in the heavens that bring winter and summer to mortal men, the constellations, when they wane, when they rise.
Eschyle

Your mother is so stupid that when she plays with the dog she is the one who runs after the ball!
Jacques Essebag

I think we are drawn to dogs because they are the uninhibited creatures we might be if we weren't certain we know better.

George Bird Evans

When your dog jumps on to your bed, this is because he loves your company. When your cat jumps on to your bed, this is because he loves your bed.

Alisha Everett

Better to live one day as a lion than an eternity as a dog.

Philip José Farmer

How many people live a dog's life that would seem more valuable if they became enraged.

Henri Fauconnier

The constable probably made a gesture, because the unfortunate Spaniel in his arms began to bark violently, trying to bite.

Frank Ferrand

The constable took the little dog in his arms and caressed him roughly.

Frank Ferrand

The king watched the constable who was playing near the fire with a small dog.

Frank Ferrand

Watch dogs or birds, for a long time, for hours if you can. You end up feeling they are always radiant. Their minds are less treacherous than ours; it does not seek to mislead them permanently.

Frank Ferrand

In dogs' heaven maybe,
Your long nose to the window,
You'll welcome us

Jean Ferrat

Lo, when two dogs are fighting in the streets,
With a third dog one of the two dogs meets;
With angry teeth he bites him to the bone,
And this dog smarts for what that dog has done.

Henry Fielding

The hair ball blocking the drain of the shower reminded Laura she would never see her little dog Pritzi again.

Claudia Fields

Anyone who hates dogs and kids can't be all that bad.

W. C. Fields

Originally, Adam and Eve were as happy as one can be when there is no work to do, no income tax, no lawyer, no doctor, no child, no dog.
W. C. Fields

Matignon, it's a dog's job.
François Fillon

Dogs have one drawback: they believe in men.
Elian J. Finbert

The cat was nursing puppies and her own kittens, and the bitch, conversely, did the same. So that we could see the kittens follow the bitch and puppies, the cat.
Elian J. Finbert

Almost everybody can be imagined as either a cat or a dog.
F. Scott Fitzgerald

*Dog. Specially created to save the life of his master
The friend of man because he is his devoted slave.*
Gustave Flaubert

Others defended themselves bitterly, and were knocked down from a distance with stones, like mad dogs.
Gustave Flaubert

The watchdogs in their kennels barked, dragging at their chains.
Gustave Flaubert

What awful winter! I saw the Seine at Rouen completely frozen, it is only the third time that in my long career I have enjoyed this hyperborean sight.
Gustave Flaubert

A teacher taught his students the art of training dogs and training hawks.
Gustave Flaubert

Boy, let this puppy out, he's just peed on the floor. Only your Lord's mastiff is entitled to enter the castle, you know.
Ken Follett

Dogs and rats behave just as nature intended. It is humans who disgust me.
Ken Follett

Ellen grew up in an almost entirely male house. She cut her hair, wore a dagger and learned not to play with kittens nor worry about the old blind dogs.
Ken Follett

For the same reason that we protect a mad dog because he barks intruders away.
Ken Follett

There floated into the room a rather strong smell which must have come from the carpet or the dog, or both.
Ken Follett

Nelly came out of the kitchen and stood near the door wagging his tail, hoping with the incurable optimism of dogs that somebody would take him to walk.
Ken Follett

She was a lady. She could play with a puppy, but if by chance he bit her, she sent him into exile in the courtyard.
Ken Follett

The dog began to work with terrible fury. As the rats were showered on him, his jaws closed again and again at a steady rhythm. He took one, broke his back with a huge jolt of his huge head and dropped it to deal with another.
Ken Follett

When no meeting was held, the owner threw a cat into the duck pond and let four dogs go at it, a game that caused great laughter among the drinkers.
Ken Follett

You can bet on dogs or rats. And if you think the rats are winning, you can bet on how many will remain when the dog is dead.
Ken Follett

Every dog should have at his side a well educated person who, at night, replaces his blanket, or serves him his dinner when he comes home as tired as a human.
Corey Ford

Henry: That's his name. Henry Jones, Junior. Indiana? We named the dog Indiana.
Harrison Ford

There are only two rules. One is E. M. Forster's guide to Alexandria; the best way to know Alexandria is to wander aimlessly. The second is from the Psalms; grin like a dog and run about through the city.
E.M. Forster

My bulldog, I love him because he is my image, a broken big mouth. In addition, he is awfully funny.

                                                                Florence Foresti

My little joy, my luck
My hair ball, my stink
My surprise, my sweetness,
My open mouth, my box of fleas,
My itch, my outbursts of laughter,
My four-pawed son, my tears,
My stomach, my alarm clock,
My noise at night, my fun,
My alibi, my wound,
My pyoderma, my polar bear
My sick angel, my big pig,
My pantry, my love,
My stick in the wheel,
My rogue, my smile,
My whoopee cushion,
My adored herpes,
My tooth, my testicles, my balls,
My insomnia, my mustache,
My poop bag, my sniff,
My dog
I love you for ever and ever.
Your amputated mistress

                                                                Florence Foresti

Consider it : a metaphysician who has to build the world as a system, only has the sophisticated cries of monkeys and dogs to build upon.
                                                                Anatole France

He had a confused vision of human cattle getting driven and letting themselves drive, in the eyes of the dog, along with their tireless dull sweetness.
                                                                Anatole France

Miraut, our dog, has turned my spit for fourteen years... His only reward for his job is to lick the pan. But he is getting old. His paw is becoming stiff, he can't see and is no longer any good at turning the spit.
                                                                Anatole France

The dog is a religious animal. In his savage state he worships the moon and the lights that float upon the waters. These are his gods to whom he appeals at night with long-drawn howls.

They trained these wretched people as fighting dogs.

Anatole France

Until one has loved an animal, part of one's soul remains unawakened.
Anatole France

A dog, I will maintain, is a very tolerable judge of beauty, as appears from the fact that any liberally educated dog does, in general, prefer a woman to a man.
Frances

Three things are better here than in the whole kingdom: men, dogs, wine.
François Ier, king of France

If you don't mind throwing tennis balls for eternity, I do have an entry into doggies' heaven.
Frank and Ernest

Don't think of hunting two hares with one dog.
Benjamin Franklin

There are three faithful friend : an old wife, an old dog, and ready money.
Benjamin Franklin

Dogs love their friends and bite their enemies, quite unlike people, who are incapable of pure love and always have to mix love and hate in their relations.
Sigmund Freud

Money will buy you a fine dog, but only love can make it wag its tail.
Richard Friedman

When two people are very much attached to each other witnesses shed a tear; when it is two dogs, it is simply a bucketful of water.
Claude Frisoni

The old dog barks backward without getting up. I can remember when he was a pup.
Robert Frost

The best feeling I have ever had about dogs came in a primitive Akah village in the mountains of northern Thailand. The Akahs keep dogs the way we keep chickens and pigs. They treat their cattle as useful working companions, give them names and would never, ever think of eating one. But they eat dogs. They are not pets - dogs are simply food. There are other ways to look at dogs. I am embarrassed by how people talk to dogs. I wonder what dogs must think. You know what I mean. You have heard it. Even dogs think it is weird. Watch a dog when a human does this. The dog cannot believe what he is hearing, either. Does Poochie wantum drinky? No. Poochie wantum go outside.

The name is not important anymore - it's the tone that counts. I feel like an old dog I know. He will come whatever name you call him, just so long as your demeanor carries with it the promise of affection and food.
Robert Fulghum

A woman, a dog and a walnut tree, the more you beat them, the better they be.
Thomas Fuller

This is the story of Wouaf wouaf-Sarko, Aquarius dog, and Mew de Villepin, Scorpion cat...
Audray Gaillard

Anyone walking his dog is at the end of the leash.
Serge Gainsbourg

Fillon's dog is called Chirac.
Gala

A gifted director can give talent to a dog. I am sure that Lassie was a very common dog.
Michel Galabru

I have a lot of diabetes, so my dog follows me wherever I go.
Michel Galabru

Men are like dogs, they come when called. Women are like cats, just call them and they will go away.
Michel Galabru

Often, the saddest thing when you leave your wife, is to leave your dog.
Michel Galabru

There is the little matter of disposing of droppings in which the cat is far ahead of his rivals. The dog is somehow thrilled by what he or any of his friends have produced, hates to leave it, adores smelling it, and sometimes eats it...The cat covers it up if he can...
Paul Gallico

Men have shaped dogs to their will. Cats are exactly as they were about ten million years ago.
Marion Garretty

He told me it was the most dangerous time being on the road at dusk, before night had quite fallen, daylight had vanished and darkness was complete.
Romain Gary

People have always been amazed at my excessive love for dogs they have this in common with us that they do not know what happens to them. We respond to this ignorance with masterpieces and they by wagging their tails.
Romain Gary

Dogs are out of fashion, men need elephants.
Romain Gary

Reform yes, shambles no.
Charles de Gaulle

The things I want to make known and find important, I ponder them for a long time, I write them all, I learn them by heart, I work long and hard, I have a hell of a job and I recite them to myself because I want them to be known. That is important. Those are the only things that have importance to me.
Charles de Gaulle

About fifty dogs chasing him were no little spur to his poor natural velocity.
Théophile Gautier

Man's nature is made up of four elements, which produce in him four attributes, namely, the beastly, the brutal, the satanic, and the divine. In man there is something of the pig, the dog, the devil, and the saint.
al-Ghazzali

In China, people do not abandon their dog when they go on vacation. They rather use it as a hot dog.
Philippe Geluck (Le Chat)

I knew a guy who was very affectionate towards his dog and the dog returned his love, he was very doggy with his master.
Philippe Geluck (Le Chat)

I do not know if the dog is my most faithful friend. But it is the only friend who brings me the sticks that I throw at it.
Philippe Geluck (Le Chat)

Dogs wag their tails when they are happy. fish also wag their tail but it drives them forward. What we cannot know is whether they are happy to advance.
Philippe Geluck (Le Chat)

Yours, mine, mine, yours? - If you loved me quite well, - You would say: The books, The dog and Our roses.
Paul Géraldy

According to Zysla Bellia, cats prefer Ruquier and Delarue to Drucker. Normal, deep within Drucker, there is his dog Olga
Valérie Ghezail

A dog biscuit cools your breath and helps prevent tartar.
Mel Gibson

She It was who cast her dog meat scraps, rather than let her boys finish them.
André Gide

During bouts of depression I am only too familiar with, like those that I have been through, I am ashamed of myself, I disclaim myself, deny myself and, like a wounded dog, brush against the walls and go hiding.
André Gide

The dog kissed the pope! But it's not my fault!
Terry Gilliam

They kissed each other's noses like puppies.
Jean Giono

You think you're stronger than one of my old hussars, said Angelo. They eat polenta with wine whenever they are in a squall.
Jean Giono

The difference between a woman and a dog lies in the price of the necklace.
François Giraudo

Any dog, without his true name, loses weight...
Giraudoux

An enlightened person - by perceiving God in all things- looks at a learned person, an outcast, even a cow, an elephant, or a dog with an equal eye.
Bhagavad Gita

This rage - I have never forgotten it - contained every anger, every revolt I had ever felt in my life - the way I felt when I saw the black dog hunted, the way I felt when I watched old Uncle Henry taken away to the almshouse, the way I felt whenever I had seen people or animals hurt for the pleasure or profit of others.
Ellen Glasgow

Ouch! A dog... a big dog full of teeth that mistook my ass for a leg of mutton!
Godi + Zidrou (l'élève Ducobu)

For their loyalty, for their kindness dogs often make us humans blush,.
Joseph Goebbels

A small dog he has been given is now frolicking in his room. The dog has conquered his heart; he can do what he pleases in the Führer's bunker. Now, this little beast is closer to the heart of the Führer than anyone else.
Joseph Goebbels

*And in that town a dog was found
As many dogs there are,
At once mongrels puppies, whelps, and hounds,
And curs of low degree.*
Oliver Goldsmith

*The dog, to gain his private ends
Went mad, and bit the man.
The man recovered from the bite
The dog it was that died.*
Oliver Goldsmith

*The watch-dog's voice that bay'd at the whispering wind,
And the loud laugh that bespoke the vacant mind.*
Oliver Goldsmith

This cat's glance, deep, mysteriously inquisitive, almost disturbing in its fixity, this eye open on you like a machine that takes your picture, makes us think that cats are better at judging the people who approach them than dogs are.
Edmond and Jules de Goncourt

We speak to a woman, saying sentences that we know she does not understand, as when we talk to a dog or a cat.
Edmond and Jules de Goncourt

The dazed man looked down the reddish mass which oozed slowly from the wound, slipping out of his body like an undulating reptile. His own bowels, doomed to end in the mud like a vulgar cheap cut intended to feed the dogs.
Terry Goodkind

He has each of the attributes of a dog except loyalty.
Senator Thomas P. Gore

Cats are the ultimate narcissists. You can tell this by all the time they spend on personal grooming. Dogs aren't like this. A dog's idea of personal grooming is to roll over a dead fish.
James Gorman

I have not too smart a dog so he does not consider me as an idiot.
Jean-Marie Gourio

There's no dog more faithful than those dogs, it is a real pain to abandon them!
Jean-Marie Gourio

Tired and fed up, dogs come home to their kennels silently at night, because nothing is better than sleep. We must sleep, since we must live.
Rémy de Gourmont

The days passed slowly, one by one
I fed the ducks, reproved my wife,
Played Handel's Largo on the fife
Or gave the dog a run.
Harry Graham

Jesse has a new dog. You may have noticed that his former pets have been peculiarly unfortunate. When this dog dies every employee in the White House will be discharged at once.
Ulysses Grant

The more I know men and the more I love my dog.
Fernand Gravey

A dog that runs out of love for life is personified happiness.
Peter Gray

A dog will forgive you quicker than any human.
Peter Gray

My goal in life is to become as wonderful as my dog thinks I am.
Toby & Eileen Green

When performing a variety of intellectually demanding tasks, cats usually emerge as clear winners (over dogs).
Dr. David Greene

Life is like a team of dogs. If you ain't the lead dog, the scenery never changes.
Lewis Grizzard

I fell concerned and depreciated by the bitchiness of all these women who are females first before being human beings.
Benoîte and Flora Groult

We lock up in a jail nothing else than a part of ourselves, as others drop on the roadside their cumbersome memories or their dogs in disgrace...
Jean-Pierre Guéno

THE DOG'S COLD NOSE

When Noah, perceiving 'twas time to embark
Persuaded the creatures to enter the Ark
The dog, with a friendliness truly sublime
Assisted in herding them.
Two at a time He drove in the elephants, zebras and gnus
Until they were packed like a boxful of screws,
The cat in the cupboard, the mouse on the shelf,
The bug in the crack; then he backed in himself.
But such was the lack of available space
He couldn't tuck all of him into the place;
So after the waters had flooded the plain
And down from the heavens fell blankets of rain
He stood with his muzzle thrust out through the door
The whole forty days of that terrible pour!
Because of which drenching, zoologists hold,
The nose of a healthy dog always is cold!

Arthur Guiterman

LITTLE LOST PUP

He was lost! not a shade of doubt of that;
For he never barked at a slinking cat,
But stood in the square where the wind blew raw
With a drooping ear and a trembling paw
And a mournful look in his pleading eye
And a plaintive sniff at the passer-by
That begged as plain as a tongue could sue,
O Mister! please may I follow you?
A lorn wee waif of a tawny brown
Adrift in the roar of a heedless town.
Oh, the saddest of sights in a world of sin
Is a little lost pup with his tail tucked in!
Now he shares my board and he owns my bed,
And he fairly shouts when he hears my tread;
Then, if things go wrong, as they sometimes do,
He asserts his right to assuage my woes
With a warm, red tongue and a nice, cold nose
And a silky head on my arm or knee
And a paw as soft as a paw can be.
When we rove the woods for a league about
He's as full of pranks as a school let out;
For he romps and frisks like a three months' colt,

And he runs me down like a thunderbolt.
Oh, the blithest of sights in the world so fair
Is a gay little pup with his tail in the air!

Arthur Guiterman

The dog's lack of pride, his meanness and fear caused him to be chosen by man, among all other animals, to be faithful, that is to say servile, to enable him to exercise his tyranny without any control and to defend him by his yells. His yelling at the approach of danger, is a warning to man and demonstrate the dog's lack of courage. The dog does not defend man: he calls to him for aid.

Sacha Guitry

Women are charming, but dogs are so loyal.

Sacha Guitry

The schedule of my dog is undoubtedly very busy, sleep-eat-play-sleep-eat-sleep, what amazes me is that it never gets confused...

Vincent Gury

A dog thinks with his nose.

Didier Hallépée

Biometric identification is changing: fingerprint, retinal scan, heart rate, venous network of the hand, typing speed... We know how to implement an increasingly large number of innovative technologies. Soon we may even identify the individual from his bodily odours. Advanced technology will finally tie us with our dog. There will just remain to store him on a chip!

Didier Hallépée

The dogs of Hell were yelling at life, terrorizing the damned souls of the masters who had abandoned them!

Didier Hallépée

Dog out, dog in, dog out, dog in... I dreamed of palace life and here I am the porter of King Charles!

Didier Hallépée

Asking a working writer what he thinks about critics is like asking a lamp-post how it feels about dogs.

Christopher Hampton

Better not take a dog on the space shuttle, because if he sticks his head out when you're coming home his face might burn up.

Jack Handy

I hope, if dogs ever take over the world and they choose a king, that they won't just go by the size, because I bet there are some Chihuahuas with good ideas.
Jack Handy

If the masses of men were one-half as faithful to God and obedient to His commands as a dog is faithful to his master and obedient to his commands - we would have a far better world to live in than we have found as yet.
R. B. Harris

In my days, we didn't have dogs or cats. All I had was Silver Beauty, my beloved paper clip.
Jennifer Hart

Women and cats will do as they please, and men and dogs should relax and get used to the idea.
Robert Heinlein

In modern war you will die like a dog for no good reason.
Ernest Hemingway

Love me, love my dog.
Henri IV, king of France

As there is something of the dog and the cat in each sex, we have to be alternately dog with cats and cat with dogs.
Marie-Jean Hérault de Séchelles

Don't let's go to the dogs tonight, for mother will be there.
Sir Alan Patrick Herbert

A rabid dog must be killed before he causes greater damage. These people were rabid dogs.
Brian Herbert & Kevin J. Anderson

Running with his dogs, he was so completely absorbed in hunting that he almost forgot the painful memories accumulated in his life.
Brian Herbert & Kevin J. Anderson

The dogs of his pack could run for hours through the heather until they flushed out a marsh hare; they then began to hunt in a joyful chorus of barking.
Brian Herbert & Kevin J. Anderson

The powerfully muscled dogs had green eyes with hints of gold, bright and set very wide apart, which gave them as piercing a sight as that of an eagle.
Brian Herbert & Kevin J. Anderson

The excitement of hunting could be read in their every movement.
Brian Herbert & Kevin J. Anderson

He that lies with the dogs, riseth with fleas.
George Herbert

When a dog is drowning, everyone offers him a drink.
George Herbert

A cat is a pygmy lion who loves mice, hates dogs, and patronizes human beings.
Oliver Herford

A woman tells lies as fast as a dog licks a plate.
John Heywood

I pray thee, let me and my fellow have a hair of the dog that bit us last night.
John Heywood

Love me, love my dog.
John Heywood

He is my other eyes that can see above the clouds; my other ears that hear above the winds. He is the part of me that can reach out into the sea. He has told me a thousand times over that I am his reason for being; by the way, he rests against my leg; by the way, he thumps his tail at my smallest smile; by the way, he shows his hurt when I leave without taking him. (I think it makes him sick with worry when he is not along to care for me.) When I am wrong, he is delighted to forgive. When I am angry, he clowns to make me smile. When I am happy, he is joy unbounded. When I am a fool, he ignores it. When I succeed, he brags. Without him, I am only another man. With him, I am all-powerful. He is loyalty itself. He has taught me the meaning of devotion. With him, I know a secret comfort and a private peace. He has brought me understanding where before I was ignorant. His head on my knee can heal my human hurts. His presence by my side is protection against my fears of dark and unknown things. He has promised to wait for me... whenever... wherever - in case I need him. And I expect I will - as I always have. He is just my dog.
Gene Hill

Nobody can fully understand the meaning of love unless he's owned a dog. He can show you more honest affection with a flick of his tail than a man can gather through a lifetime of handshakes.
Gene Hill

Whoever said you can't buy happiness forgot about puppies.
Gene Hill

When you are going to die, all the animals that you knew will come and form a chain to hoist you into the sky.
Hindu legend

I am an animal lover and I especially love dogs. What wonderful creatures: intelligent, attached to their master, brave, sensitive and beautiful! A guide dog is one of the most touching things around. He is more attached to man than any other of his kind. If he is off to meet a female friend, he returns immediately with a bad conscience.
Adolphe Hitler

I was desperate. The swine who stole my dog doesn't realize what he did to me!
Caporal Hitler, 1917

In order to really enjoy a dog, one doesn't merely try to train him to be semi-human. The point of it is to open oneself to the possibility of becoming partly a dog.
Edward Hoagland

By and large, people who enjoy teaching animals to roll over will find themselves happier with a dog.
Barbara Holland

A dog is not almost human, and I know of no greater insult to the canine race than to describe it as such.
John Holmes

Lush! Dog's eye and deer's heart!
Homère

You may have a dog that won't sit up, roll over or even cook breakfast, not because she's too stupid to learn how to but because she's too smart to bother.
Rick Horowitz

If the dog embodies action, the cat is rather a symbol of reflection.
Marie-Luce Hubert

Reigning is the art of getting dogs to walk standing and men on all fours.
Victor Hugo

The dog's smile is in his tail.
Victor Hugo

The dog is virtue that, being unable to become man, chose to become a beast.
Victor Hugo

The stupidest place you can poke your nose into is a muzzle. At least dogs do so by force; a man is stupid enough to do so voluntarily, the day he marries.
Victor Hugo

Look your dog in the eye and you will not say he has no soul.
Victor Hugo

By living with his pet, the child will gain many human qualities that he will keep as an adult. The animal allows him to develop his personality, his sense of responsibility, responds to his emotional needs and his desire to communicate. The animal is also a consolation in any conflict with his parents or his friends at school. His four-legged friend accepts him for what he is and does not judge him. He is a confidant to whom he can tell everything and who helps him to reduce his anxiety in difficult situations.
François Hugues

Our familiar companions, these "love machines", are consumed by the intensity of the love they give us. The strength of their feelings, of their passion does not tally with a longer life.
Jean-Pierre Hutin

When a dog or cat is already very old, I recommend taking another, a younger one.
Reha Hutin

When you have long lived with an animal, you finally know it.
Reha Hutin

The President (Valery Giscard d'Estaing) ran on all fours, distributing the bowls to puppies, you could see he liked it.
Reha Hutin

To his dog, every man is Napoleon; hence the constant popularity of dogs.
Aldous Huxley

There are times when even the best manager is like the little boy with the big dog, waiting to see where the dog wants to go so he can take him there.
Lee Iacocca

You learn things in business: If you want a friend, get a dog.
Carl Celian Icahn

My dog is usually pleased with what I do, because she is not infected with the concept of what I should be doing.
Lonzo Idolswine

I can imagine a cat changes himself to a philosopher, but a dog does not.
Hajime Irisawa

A barking dog is often more useful than a sleeping lion.
Washington Irving

Texas is a fine place for men and dogs, but hell for women and horses.
Mary Ivins

Man is a dog's idea of what God should be.
Holbrook Jackson

Starve your dog, he will follow you. Fatten him, he will eat you.
Abu Jafar al-Mansur

*I am bored, pick girls for me
and blue irises in the shade of elms...
These lines I am doing bother me too
and my dog is starting to squint, sitting,
listening to the clock
that bores him as much as I am bored.*
Francis Jammes

Gluttonous, womanizer, evil, cowardly, mangy, in short, my late dog was almost a man.
Jules Janin

In summer, dogs, overwhelmed by the heat, sleep like grape harvesters, their tail between their paws.
Jean-Charles

What strange yarns is the web of affections made of! I saw a man pay attention to another only because the latter had praised the name of his dog, or because both had a taste for the same foods or the same wines, or had the same tailor. Finally, the smallest similarities, which often have no other cause than chance or the most material tastes, sometimes make men closer and more closely united than the main features of their characters.
Jean-Paul II

Animals have a soul.
Jean-Paul II

It is very imprudent, a dog; he never makes it his business to inquire whether you are in the right or the wrong, never asks whether you are rich or poor, silly or wise, sinner or saint. You are his pal. That is enough for him.
Jérôme Klapka Jérôme

Let your boat of life be light, packed with only what you need - a homely home and simple pleasures, one or two friends worth the name, someone to love and someone to love you, a cat, a dog, and a pipe or two, enough to eat and enough to wear, and a little more than enough to drink; for thirst is a dangerous thing.
Jérôme Klapka Jérôme

No matter whether you're wrong or right, lucky or not, rich or poor, educated or uneducated, holy or fisherman. You are his friend and that is enough. He will always be near you to comfort you, protect you and will even sacrifice his life for you. It will serve you in good times and bad. It's your wife, your husband? No, only your dog.
Jérôme Klapka Jérôme

Dogs never talk about themselves but listen to you while you talk about yourself, and keep up an appearance of being interested in the conversation.
Jérôme Klapka Jérôme

Romance, like the rabbit at the dog track, is the elusive, never attained fake reward which, for the benefit and amusement of our masters, keeps us running and thinking in safe circles.
Beverly Jones

Scratch a dog and you'll find a permanent job.
Franklin P Jones

I do honour the very flea of his dog.
Ben Jonson

Hell hound on my trail.
Robert Johnson

I do not know, sir, that the fellow is an infidel; but if he be an infidel, he is an infidel as a dog is an infidel; that is to say, he has never thought upon the subject.
Samuel Johnson

I would rather see the portrait of a dog that I know, than all the allegorical paintings they can show me in the world.
Samuel Johnson

Sir, a woman preaching is like a dog walking on his hind legs. It is not done well; but you are surprised to find it done at all.
Samuel Johnson

When a dog barks at the moon, then it is religion; but when he barks at strangers, it is patriotism!

David Starr Jordan

He's fair. He treats us all the same way - like dogs.
Henry Jordan

A Dominican inquisitor in the mid-thirteenth century, Etienne de Bourbon, one day in confession is informed that women of the Dombes are bearing sickly children to the grave of a saint Guinefort. Having made inquiries, the Dominicannoticed with amazement that it was actually a greyhound unjustly killed by his master, a knight. He had left her child alone with the dog in his castle. A large snake came into the house and crept to the cradle, but the dog managed to kill him. When the knight returned, he found his dog's blood, and he then thought that he had devoured the child. Without thinking, he executed him. Realizing his mistake then, he buried the beast near the castle into a well and planted trees in remembrance of the faithful animal. But "the castle was destroyed by the divine will and the earth brought back to desert state". Farmers who have heard the story of the dog honoured him as a martyr, able to work miracles for too weak children.
Philippe Joutard

I see the regions of snow and ice, I see the sharp-eyed Samoiede and the Finn, I see the seal-seeker in his boat poising his lance, I see the Siberian on his slight-built sledge drawn by dogs, I see the porpoise-hunters, I see the whale-crews of the south Pacific and the north Atlantic, I see the cliffs, glaciers, torrents, valleys of Switzerland - I mark the long winters and the isolation.
James Joyce

Snob: man who sends his dog to London to learn barking.
Philippe Jullian

Do not tread on the tail of my dog!
Patricia Kaas

All knowledge, the totality of all questions and all answers is contained in the dog.
Kafka

And having to fit into a country that is already its own, it is smelling, biting tail, so keeping up a dog status
José Kaminsky

Nobody more than me has the right to tell the truth about dogs. I owned a beautiful Newfoundland dog for ten years; between us, the ordinary relations were reversed: I was subjected, humble, faithful as a dog; He was moody, weird, awkward as a man. It was me who was his friend.

Well, after a ten years' association, he undertook twice to devour me and forced me to sum up our friendship as well: 1° dogs are no better than men; 2° my dog loved me like you love steak.
Alphonse Karr

In case of danger from rats, grasshoppers, birds or insects, appropriate animals (cats, mongooses) will be released and these predators must be protected against the risk of being killed or attacked by dogs.
Kautilya (Arthashastra)

The daily ration for an Arya man is one prastha of rice, one quarter prastha of bread, one kuduba of oil or butter and one quarter kuduba of salt. For a non-Aryan, a prastha of rice, one sixth prastha of bread, one half-kuduba of oil and one quarter kuduba of salt. [...] For a dog, one prastha of rice.
Kautilya (Arthashastra)

Whoever has stolen or killed a small animal (rooster, cat, dog, pig) of a value of less than 25 panas will have the nose cut or pay a fine of 54 panas.
Kautilya (Arthashastra)

Dogs don't lie and why should they? Strangers come, they growl and bark, they know their loved ones in the dark, Now let me, by night or day, be just as full of truth as they.
Garrison Keillor

Man tries to swallow meaning whole as a dog would eat his dinner.
Walt Kelly

Women are like cats and dogs. If you can attract any cat and make any dog listen to you, you can have any women you like.
Frederik Kerling

A sound as of a cornered-animal's fear and hate and surrender and defiance... like the last sound the shot falling animal makes as the dogs get him, when he finally doesn't care about anything but himself and his dying.
Ken Kesey

The dog's tail will always be bent, even a hundred times fitted into a mold.
Sahar Khalifa

What we can we will be,
Honest Englishmen.
Do the work that's nearest,
Though it's dull at times,

Helping, when we meet them,
Lame dogs over stiles.

Charles Kingsley

When all the world is young, lad,
And all the trees are green;
And every goose a swan, lad,
And every lass a queen;
Then hey for boot and horse, lad,
And round the world away:
Young blood must have its course, lad,
And every dog his day.

Charles Kingsley

Brothers and Sisters, I bid you beware of giving your heart to a dog to tear.

Rudyard Kipling

Politics are not my concern... they impressed me as a dog's life without a dog's decencies.

Rudyard Kipling

When the Man waked up he said,
'What is Wild Dog doing here?'
And the Woman said,
'His name is not Wild Dog any more,
But the First Friend,
Because he will be our friend
For ever and ever and ever.'

Rudyard Kipling

_ What's the point of keeping a paralyzed dog?
_ It's decorative. It's like a rug, but alive.

Cédric Klapisch

But it's far too luxurious for a dog!

Cédric Klapisch

No doubt, the dog is faithful. But must we, because of this, take example from him? He is faithful to man, not to the dog.

Karl Kraus

Although surrounded by sincere friends, the hare was eaten by dogs.

Ignacy, comte Krasicki

This is rat eat rat, dog eat dog. I'll kill 'em, and I'm going to kill 'em before they kill me. Speaking of competition in the fast-food industry.

Ray Kroc

Dogs are our link to paradise. They don't know evil or jealousy or discontent. To sit with a dog on a hillside on a glorious afternoon is to be back in Eden, where doing nothing was not boring--it was peace.
Milan Kundera

A dog is like a liberal, he wants to please everybody. A cat doesn't really need to know that everybody loves him.
William Kunstler

Pomeranians speak only to Poodles and Poodles speak only to God.
Charles Kuralt

Chase a dog away from the king's chair, he climbs on to the preacher's chair.
Jean de La Bruyère

A Wolf had only bones and skin,
So watchful the dogs were.
Jean de La Fontaine

His brother, who ran many a high adventure,
Put many a Stag at bay, many a Boar slaughtered,
was the first Caesar that the dog tribe had had.
Jean de La Fontaine

Snarling dog always has torn ear.
Jean de La Fontaine

Strange! We teach temperance to dogs, and we cannot teach it to men!
Jean de La Fontaine

The dog, seeing his prey in the water represented,
Left it for the picture, and all but drowned;
The river became suddenly agitated.
With great difficulty he returned to the bank
And got neither the shadow nor the body.
Jean de La Fontaine

Phantasm of barking like a dog to distract people from the track.
Jacques Lacan

The dog goes mew mew, the cat goes Wah-Wah.
Jacques Lacan

Oh, this is only a dog!
Jacques Lacan

A dog is only a dog!
Jacques Lacan

The more I see of the representatives of the people, the more I admire my dogs.
Alphonse de Lamartine

Know yourself. Don't accept your dog's admiration as conclusive evidence that you are wonderful.
Ann Landers

If he were a dog, they would say that he is strictly obedient. But because he is a man, they say that it is experience.
Gilbert Langlois

What fascinates us in the cat is precisely that he is beyond the reach of the clumsy logic of the dog and to provide him with hugs and treats is not enough to put him in one's pocket.
Jacques Lanzmann

Understanding a dog is within reach of everyone. His yelps, his attitudes are as eloquent as a long speech. However, understanding a cat is more complex.
Jacques Lanzmann

Heaven and earth are neither humane nor as benevolent as men, they treat all beings as if they were straw dogs used in sacrifices.
Lao-Tseu

I will talk about the third woman in the house, the one that has crept between Do and me for four years. I refer of course to Therese: the backstage star, the longhaired pinup, the top model of Spaniels and so on.
Catherine Lara

It's nice, a man in a house. If you think of it, it is even better than a dog.
Gérard Lauzier

A man without a friend, it is worse than a homeless dog.
Stephen Lawhead

We talked tonight, Valette and I, about this scratching of clothes with their hands that all the dying have, or almost all of them. I told him that animals do the same, at least dogs and cats, of which I saw many die. A dog, a cat, at the moment of death, if they are in a garden, scratch the ground with their forepaws, if they are in a house, scratch the floor, if they are on a bed, scratch the bed on which they are. What does this gesture mean, this movement, that both humans and animals have? It probably has the same animal origin, purely instinctive.
Paul Léautaud

If you are a dog and your owner suggests that you wear a sweater...suggest that he wears a tail.
Fran Lebowitz

This Averroes dog said: intelligence puts universality in things.
Jacques Lefèvre d'Etaples

The deer only like china dogs.
Jacky Legge

You never knew, philosopher, oh old brother,
The silly noisy loyalty of the dog.
You love me, however, and my heart does feel it.
Jules Lemaître

When a dog wags his tail and barks at the same time, how do you know which end to believe?
Barry Levinson

But the animal has no veil.
Dogs better treated than Afghan women?
Charles de Leusse

But the dog who is rabid
Is not by bowl attracted.
Charles de Leusse

Who has a dog
Doesn't bark.
Charles de Leusse

When a dog mews
It's because he eats him.
Charles de Leusse

A dog thinks: Hey, these people I live with feed me, love me, provide me with a nice warm, dry house, pet me, and take good care of me... They must be Gods! A cat thinks: Hey, these people I live with feed me, love me, provide me with a nice warm, dry house, pet me, and take good care of me... I must be a God!
Ira Lewis

Praying to the sun is something forgivable. Everyone looks unintentionally to a bright place, animals do and what, in the cat or dog, is an involuntary glance towards the light is, in humans, called prayer.
Georg Christoph Lichtenberg

The dog is the most vigilant of animals, although he sleeps all day.
Georg Christoph Lichtenberg

I've been on so many blind dates, I should get a dog free.
Wendy Liebman

I care not much for the religion of a man whose dog and cat are none the better for it.
Abraham Lincoln

How many legs does a dog have if you call the tail a leg? Four. Calling a tail a leg doesn't make it a leg.
Abraham Lincoln

Better give right of way to a dog than be bitten by him in contesting for this right. Even killing the dog would not cure the bite.
Abraham Lincoln

I stand fearlessly for small dogs, the American Flag, motherhood and the Bible. That's why people love me.
Art Linkletter

Suppress from the world women, flowers and dogs, what does remain?
Hyppolite de Livry

It may kill a flea on the back of a dog 500 yards away.
Christopher Lloyd

All cats are grey in the dark.
Thomas Lodge

A bone to a dog is not charity. Charity is the bone shared with the dog, when you are just as hungry as the dog.
Jack London

Buck did not read the newspapers, or he would have known that trouble was brewing, not only for himself, but for every tidewater dog, strong of muscle and with warm, long hair, from Puget Sound to San Diego.
Jack London

Few things give me as much confidence and joy as my dog's loyalty.
Konrad Lorenz

I like dogs better than people. They give you unconditional love. They either lick your face or bite you, but you always know where they're coming from. With people, you never know which ones will bite. The difference between dogs and men is that you know where dogs sleep at night.
Greg Louganis

Cats' beauty is classical while that of Dogs is gothic.
Howard Lovecraft

Dogs are farmers and farmers' animals, cats are gentlemen and gentlemen's animals.
Howard P. Lovecraft

One proof of the superior dignity of the cat lies in our practice of using the words "cat" and "dog" to qualify a particular behaviour or attitude.
Howard P. Lovecraft

We own a dog -- he is with us as a slave and inferior because we wish him to be. But we entertain a cat -- he adorns our hearth as a guest, fellow-lodger, and equal because he wishes to be there. It is no compliment to be the stupidly idolized master of a dog, whose instinct it is to idolize, but it is a very distinct tribute to be chosen as the friend and confidant of a cat.
Howard P. Lovecraft

What kind of life is a dog's life? I have sometimes tried to imagine it by kneeling or lying full length on the ground and looking up. The world then becomes strangely incomplete; one sees little but legs.
E V Lucas

Just as one year in a dog's life is equivalent to seven years in a human life, one year in the high-technology business is like seven years in any other industry.
Regis Mac Kenna

Men are worse than dogs, whenever the devil of the flesh torments them.
Pierre Mac Orlan

The saddest thing in the world: a dog without a man. And the greatest joy that we can see on earth: a dog with a man.
Macedonion

Watching baseball under the lights is like observing dogs indoors, at a pedigree show. In both instances, the environment is too controlled to suit the species.
Melvin Maddocks

In the world which we know, among the different and primitive geniuses that preside over the evolution of the several species, there is not a single one, excepting the dog, that ever gave a thought to the presence of man.
Maurice Maeterlinck

*Small dog I attracted you
With sugar and my calves.*
Stéphane Mallarmé

Man is a dog's ideal of what God should be.

André Malraux

We are starting to suffer here, we delight in eating horse meat, the donkey is overpriced, there are dog butchers, cat butchers and rat butchers - Paris is awfully sad, when will it end?
Edouard Manet

He showed the cruelty of Duke of Berry's people due to lack of good advice, saying that there had to be traitors in the kingdom. Which a prelate named Cardinal Bar, who attended this sermon, denied and called him " wicked dog", for which he [Cardinal] was most hated by the University and the common people.
Renaud de la Marche

The Unknown is a harmless little dog that roars like a lion!
Laurent Martinez

Chicolini: My dog - believe me, he's some smart dog. You know he went with Admiral Byrd to the Pole.
Firefly: I'll bet the dog got to the pole first.
Groucho Marx

Just give me a comfortable couch, a dog, a good book, and a woman. Then, if you can get the dog to go somewhere and read the book, I might have a little fun!
Groucho Marx

Outside of a dog, a book is man's best friend. Inside of a dog, it's too dark to read.
Groucho Marx

Personally, I do not understand why a man would not have the right to have both a dog and a woman. But if you do not have the means to afford both, rather buy a dog then.
Groucho Marx

He was seized by an animal urge to scream in the manner of tied -up dogs.
Guy de Maupassant

The dislodged boar slipped, pursued by the dogs howling through the bushes.
Guy de Maupassant

Then more screams arise, shrill yelps; it is jackals that are coming, and sometimes you can only hear a stronger odd voice, that of the hyena, which imitates the dog to attract and devour him.
Guy de Maupassant

He slipped like a dog into the kitchen, eager for scraps from the food storage, lunched on the run off a carcass, a slice of tinned cold poultry, or a cluster of grapes and a crust rubbed with garlic, his only meal of the day!
François Mauriac

Like a dog barking at the moon, I was fascinated by a reflection.
François Mauriac

The evening was pulsing with the sounds of shepherds calling, dogs barking, with bursts of laughter.
François Mauriac

And if I were a dog I would be Bush, a Staff with the femur of an Iraqi in the mouth.
Médine

This isn't like naming your dog Spot.
Richard Melville

A professor must have a theory as a dog must have fleas.
H L Mencken

For men with insatiable curiosity, their prototype is not the liberator releasing slaves, the good Samaritan I helping up the fallen, but a dog sniffing tremendously at an infinite series of rat-holes.
H.L. Mencken

But the philosopher of a nation of shopkeepers is deep down more a shopkeeper than a philosopher, just as a hunting dog is not so much a hunting dog as a dog.
Henri Michaux

In England, if you do not want to be hit by a car when you push a baby carriage, attach a dog to it.
George Mikes

A dog will flatter you but you have to flatter a cat.
George Mikes

You can keep a dog; but it is the cat who keeps people, because cats find humans useful domestic animals.
George Mikes

The biggest dog has been a pup.
Joaquin Miller

To give stray dogs a home is very commendable, but not when you are up to your neck in a dangerous mission.
Karen Miller

A Pekingese is not a pet dog; he is an undersized lion.

A A Milne

I did but prompt the age to quit their clogs
By the known rules of ancient liberty,
When straight a barbarous noise environs me
Of owls and cuckoos, asses, apes and dogs.

John Milton

However I asked only little, this dog I asked him merely to become a man. It was so easy, I thought. He obstinately refused.

Octave Mirbeau

The world could be worse and fleas larger than dogs.

Jean Mistler

No argument whatsoever will justify that we should throw to the dogs the honour of a man and ultimately his life at the price of a double infringement in his accusers of the fundamental laws of our Republic, those that protect the dignity and freedom of each of us.

François Mitterrand

You 've spoken about dogs and cats, I too love them. Besides, I think we have dogs of the same race, God knows if we are fond of them... But you do not have the monopoly of the hearts of dogs and cats.

François Mitterrand

Even the worst dog of all feels mercy when killing his victim, I have no mercy when I kill an enemy. So I am not an animal.

Conquérant Mongol

In a distant age when the seas were only mud hills and mountains, God shaped the first man and first woman from clay and let a cat and a dog watch over them when he left to fetch the water of eternal life in the sources of immortality. In his absence, a demon put their vigilance to sleep by providing milk and meat and, while they were paying no attention, he urinated on the new creation of God. The latter, enraged to see the fur of his creatures made so dirty, ordered the cat to clean it with his tongue, except for the hair that was intact. The rough tongue of the cat removed all the dirty hair it could reach, leaving only a few hairs in the armpits and groin. God covered the dog with all that the cat had removed. Then he sprinkled his creatures of clay with the sacred waters of the eternal fountain but could not give them immortality because of the desecration due to the devil.

Mythologie Mongole

Some children show their dog the affection they cannot give to people. Receiving in return the love of the animal helps them to move away gradually from isolation.
Hubert Montagner

The animal can unlock the inner world of the child.
Hubert Montagner

The friendship of a dog is certainly more intense and more constant than that of Man.
Michel Eyquem de Montaigne

He was seized with great terror, and the idea of dying abandoned, helpless, like a dog in a ditch, inspired him with profound dread.
Xavier de Montépin

I love animals. First of all, I think, because they do not speak. "About the time when animals could speak..." Oh, for goodness' sake, not that! It is likely that animals are as stupid as men, they often give us reason to believe so, but their silence prevents them from competing seriously.
Henry de Montherlant

Scalded cats dread cold water.
Montluc

You may know the snappish cur by his torn ears.
Montluc

No one appreciates the very special genius of your conversation so much as the dog does.
Christopher Morley

Errare caninum est.
Morris (Rantanplan)

Artists like cats; soldiers like dogs.
Desmond Morris

There are only two rules. One is E. M. Forster's guide to Alexandria; the best way to know Alexandria is to wander about aimlessly. The second is from the Psalms; grin like a dog and run about through the city.
Jan Morris

Jean de Bethencourt so named the Canary Islands because a volcano in the vicinity of the port of Tenerife was the shape of a dog's head - canis for the Romans.
Claude Mossé

Could he foresee that a woman could have men at her bidding as the master his dogs?

Claude Mossé

Did you ever walk into a room and forget why you walked in? I think that is how dogs spend their lives.

Sue Murphy

Have doubts, if you want, about one who loves you, a woman or a dog, but not about love itself.

Alfred de Musset

What a voracious dog nothingness is? Should it take from us this short life day by day, all of which will belong to it sooner or later?

Alfred de Musset

*Dogs display reluctance and wrath
If you try to give them a bath.
They bury bones in hideaways
And half the time they trot sideways.*

Ogden Nash

Door: What a dog is perpetually on the wrong side of.

Ogden Nash

*Ten years ago she split the air
To seize what she could spy.
Tonight she bumps against a chair,
Betrayed by milky eye.
She seems to pant,
Time up, time up!
My little dog must die,
And lie in dust with Hector's pup;
So, presently, must I.*

Ogden Nash

*The dog is man's best friend.
He has a tail on one end.
Up in front he has teeth.
And four legs underneath.*

Ogden Nash

A traveler must have the back of an ass to bear all, a tongue like the tail of a dog to flatter all, the mouth of a hog to eat what is set before him, the ear of a merchant to hear all and say nothing.

Thomas Nashe

*And I, a materialist who does not believe
in the starry heaven promised
to a human being,
for this dog and for every dog,
I believe in heaven, yes, I believe in a heaven
that I will never enter, but he waits for me
wagging his big fan of a tail
so I, soon to arrive, will feel welcome.*

Pablo Neruda

*No, my dog used to watch me
giving me the attention I need,
yet only the attention necessary
to let a vain person know
that he being a dog,
with those eyes, more pure than mine,
was wasting time, but he watched
with a look that reserved for me
every bit of sweetness...*

Pablo Neruda

*O merry, merry, merry,
as only dogs know how to be happy
and nothing more, with an absolutely
shameless nature.*

Pablo Neruda

The dog laughs with his tail.

Paul Neuhuys

Remorse is, like a dog's bite at a stone __stupid.

Friedrich Nietzsche

The world was conquered through the understanding of dogs; the world exists thanks to the understanding of dogs.

Friedrich Nietzsche

Whenever I climb I am followed by a dog called 'Ego'.

Friedrich Nietzsche

Zarathustra shall not be the shepherd and the dog of a herd!

Friedrich Nietzsche

It is really confusing to think of the time people lose leafing through dictionaries, when we had the good fortune to talk for some time with a well-bred Great Dane, like the bailiff of the Isle of Man.

Charles Nodier

Dogs' lives are too short. Their only fault, really.
Carlotta Monterey O'Neill

Revenge is often like biting a dog because the dog bit you.
Austin O'Malley

It is easy to understand why the cat has eclipsed the dog as modern America's favorite pet. People like pets to possess the same qualities that they do. Cats are irresponsible and recognize no authority, yet are completely dependent on others for their material needs. Cats cannot be made to do anything useful. Cats are mean for the fun of it. In fact, cats possess so many of the same qualities as some people that it is often hard to tell people and cats apart.
P.J. O'Rourke

People are all exactly alike. There's no such thing as a race and barely such a thing as an ethnic group. If we were dogs, we'd be the same breed. George Bush and an Australian Aborigine have fewer differences than a Lhasa Apso and a Toy Fox Terrier. A Japanese raised in Riyadh would be an Arab. A Zulu raised in New Rochelle would be an orthodontist. People are all the same, though their circumstances differ terribly.
P.J. O'Rourke

Looking for a dog is more difficult than finding a Secretary of Commerce.
Obama

We are worried, apparently, these dogs love to eat tomatoes. And Michelle has a garden where she grows tomatoes. I think the garden is in danger.
Obama

To a dog happiness is what lies on the other side of a door.
Charleton Ogburn Jr.

Asking a writer what he thinks about critics is like asking a lamppost what it feels about dogs.
John Osborne

A boar is often held by a not-so-large dog. - A cane non magno saepe tenetur aper
Ovide

Any member introducing a dog into the Society's premises shall be liable to a fine of one pound. Any animal leading a blind person shall be deemed to be a cat.
Oxford Union Society

The cat lets Man support her. But unlike the dog, he is no hand licker. Furthermore, unlike Man's other great good friend, the horse, the cat is no sweating serf of Man. The only labor he condescends to perform is to catch mice and rats, and that's fun.
Vance Packard

A dog, when he is hit by a stone, tries to bite the stone rather than the one who threw it.
Pacuvius

It is sometimes difficult to know who, in a family, is in command: husband, wife, mother-in-law or cook. But the house dog is never wrong.
Marcel Pagnol

Single women are like goats without a dog, they only make bullshits.
Marcel Pagnol

The reader is as ungrateful as a cat. The cat, who is a very intelligent animal, is not ungrateful, but he knows he should not rely on writers who love only dogs. Do not feel concerned about cats or dogs, but about the country's problems.
Orhan Pamuk

A dog emerged from behind a barrel of rainwater and, his hair bristling, began to bark against the invader. A soldier killed him with a spear.
Christopher Paolini

On several occasions, outraged dogs charged down at them, giving tongue, ready to defend their territory against invaders... Very proud of their success and wagging tail, the hounds returned to the kennel, the barn, the porch, where they mounted guard over their fiefdoms.
Christopher Paolini

They look like two hungry dogs fighting over a piece of meat!
Christopher Paolini

When two mangy dogs approached the dragon, barking, she looked up and growled. With their tails between their legs, the two villains fled with cries of terror.
Christopher Paolini

The conclusion I have reached is that, above all, dogs are witnesses. They are allowed access to our most private moments. They are there when we think we are alone. Think of what they could tell us. They sit on the laps of presidents. They see acts of love and violence, quarrels and feuds, and the secret play of children. If they could tell us everything they have seen, all of the gaps of our lives would stitch themselves together.
Carolyn Parkhurst

The more I see of men, the better I like my dog.
Blaise Pascal

Mine, yours. "This dog is mine, said these poor children, this is my place in the sun." This is the beginning and the image of the usurpation of the whole earth.
Blaise Pascal

Even the tiniest Poodle or Chihuahua is still a wolf at heart.
Dorothy Hinshaw Patent

Animals are the small part of God's creation, and one day we shall meet again in the mystery of Christ.
Paul VI

A dog is a dog, a bird is a bird, and a cat is a person.
Mugsy Peabody

Never stand between a dog and the hydrant.
John Peers

For the fifth year in succession I have pored over the catalogue of dogs in the show at Madison Square Garden without finding a dog named Rover, Towser, Sport, Spot or Fido.
Who is the man who can call from the back door at night: Here, Champion Alexander of Clane o' Wind-Holme! Here, Champion Alexander of Clane o' Wind-Holme?
Westbrook Pegler

There is nothing to understand or expect from us. Because we are not of your world. Do you know how to talk to dogs, cats, earthworms?
Pierre Pelot

Men are generally more careful of the lineage of their horses and dogs than of their children.
William Penn

The city is the favourite food of dogs.
Daniel Pennac

Milou... it is not a dog's name, it is a picture name.
Daniel Pennac

We think that we take our dog for a pee at noon and in the evening. Big mistake: it is the dog that invites us out twice a day for meditation.
Daniel Pennac

It's very hard not to be affected by the love and devotion of the King Charles and it is one of the reasons there is such a surge of interest in this very lovable, naughty and charming breed.

Alicia Pennington

Why is it that no other species but man gets bored? Under the circumstances in which a man gets bored, a dog goes to sleep.
Walker Percy

You can be God of the dogs, God of the cats, God of the poor, you just need a leash, some slack, some fortune, but you'll never be master of the tree. All you can ever do is want to become a tree in your turn.
Georges Perec

With the letters of his name,
The French dog builds his house:
Chien (dog) / niche (kennel);
While this is not the case
For the cat
Who has no house of his own,
Except for the alleys!
And alleys
Filled with rats: that's not very inviting!
Domi Perez

We knew Ranucci was in Marseille. He had hit a dog, and given his identity to the owner of the animal. But why has it never been mentioned? Because, replied the officer, it did not emerge until after the conclusion of the investigation.
Gilles Perrault

It has been related that dogs drink from the river Nile while running the bank along so that they may not be seized by the crocodiles.
Phèdre

Bossuet said masses for animals.
Monseigneur Dominique Philippe

When I started to bless the animals, they called me a fool.
Monseigneur Dominique Philippe

It is not uncommon for children of the queen to complain about not being able to see their mother quietly without the dogs around. Prince Philip, it is said, often finds these d… dogs intrusive!
Prince Philippe

Steps have been taken, a silent uproar has unleashed the dogs of war
Pink Floyd

The old saw about old dogs and new tricks only applies to certain people.
Daniel Pinkwater

No dog is like another.

Josiane Pirard

I descend from the wolf and I have instincts that come from time immemorial.

Josiane Pirard

The content of my bowl is mine.

Josiane Pirard

One can understand the feelings of a dog through the movement of its tail and of the rest of its body.

Josiane Pirard

When a shepherd goes to kill a wolf and takes his dog along to see the sport, he should take care to avoid some mistakes. The dog has certain relationships to the wolf the shepherd may have forgotten.

Robert M. Pirsig

The disposition of noble dogs is to be gentle with people they know and the opposite with those they don't know...How, then, can the dog be anything other than a lover of learning since it defines what is its own and what is not.

Platon

Alcibiades had a beautiful marvelous great dog that had cost him seven hundred crowns, He cut off his tail, which was the most beautiful part of his body, for which his friends scolded him, saying he had become everyone's talk, and everyone blamed him very much for having defamed a beautiful dog. He only laughed, and said: That's all I ask for. I want the Athenians to go chattering about that, so they will not speak evil of me.

Plutarque

Jacques Chirac has a complex relationship, alternating love and rejection, with Sumet, a Maltese, a gift from Michel Drucker. The former president can caress her for hours, talk about everything and nothing, then snub her for several days.

Le Point

Animal lovers are proving formidable enemies of mankind.

Michel Polac

Nothing seems better to justify the pessimism of Schopenhauer than the eye of the dog when you look at him shitting.

Michel Polac

We need concepts. We can hardly do without them. Without them we would not be able to call this table a table, this dog a dog.

Jean-Bernard Pontalis

But think, if admitted to that equal sky, his faithful dog shall bear him company.
Alexander Pope

Histories are fuller of examples of the fidelity of dogs than of friends.
Alexander Pope

How do we know that we have a right to kill creatures that we are so little above, such as dogs, for our curiosity or even for some use to us?
Alexander Pope

You are playing the part of the gardener's dog.
Jean-Baptiste Poquelin (Molière)

*Where his heart becomes attached, his court the lover pays,
To gain his friends' goodwill, his plans he lays,
And that there may be none to thwart his ends,
He strives even with the house-dog to make friends.*
Jean-Baptiste Poquelin (Molière)

*One only hears these words: dog, wolf, tart.
First their caps flew across the square
And, showing two bare heads without hair,
They made their fight laughably awful.*
Jean-Baptiste Poquelin (Molière)

He who would drown his dog first calls him mad.
Jean-Baptiste Poquelin (Molière)

It's funny how dogs and cats know the inside of folks better than other folks do, isn't it?
Eleanor H. Porter

Penelope Fillon said her dog is named Paddy like the brand of whisky.
The Post

Do not try to attack the demon head on. He would be too happy that you took care of him. Instead, treat him with contempt, like a troublesome dog which you want to get rid of.
Jean Pottier

People forgotten in the crowd are like stray dogs begging for blows to get adopted.
Jean Poutet

London is sentimental and tolerant. The attitude to foreigners is like the attitude to dogs: Dogs are neither human nor British, but so long as you

keep them under control, give them their exercise, feed them, pat them, you will find their wild emotions amusing, and their characters interesting.
V S Pritchett

Because small children and dogs who earlier watched Mr. Santeuil before they fell asleep again, do serious things with their little bodies like sleeping, like dying.
Marcel Proust

The small barking of the dog that hunted away at the other end of the horizon, awakened the barking, even lower at this distance, of the dog at the Aigneaux farm.
Marcel Proust

The dog would feast on acorns
If not attending garbage.
Of the oak the branch
Stretches skyward
Raymond Queneau

I am Mao's dog, I bite when he tells me to bite.
Jiang Qing

Run all after the dog, he will never bite you, always drink before thirst, and it will never happen to you.
François Rabelais

But I only found a horrible medley
Of bones and bruised flesh and, dragged through the mud,
Scraps full of blood, and I gory limbs
That devouring dogs fought over.
Jean Racine

I think dogs are the most amazing creatures; they give unconditional love. To my mind, they are the role model for being alive.
Gilda Radner

Using authority to maintain your power is an aberration. If you have authority over your dog, no need to hit him or even raise your voice. And if he disobeys, it is because you have already lost control. In reality, authority is exercised from the moment you have lost it.
Mikhaïl W. Ramseier

My dog is unbearable, but I keep it for sentimental reasons: my husband hates it.
Juliette Récamier

Between the dog and his master, there is only the jump of a flea.

Jules Renard

House closed. A wall. Nobody, except for a dog on the wall. To rent, contact the dog. He will welcome you.

Jules Renard

A one-eyed man is a cripple who is entitled to only half a guide dog.

Jules Renard

Our dogs will love and admire the meanest of us, and feed our colossal vanity with their uncritical homage.

Agnès Replier

You are like the dog who cries before the stone falls on him.

Reynard cycle

And life is so great a good,
That this old man, this slave, this dog,
Regrets all, he who has nothing.

Jean Richepin

In a salon, a young over-skinny woman had a superb skinny dog lying at her feet.
- Who is it? asked a lady to Rivarol.
- It's a dog guarding a bone.

comte de Rivarol

My obstetrician was so dumb that when I gave birth he forgot to cut the cord. For a year that kid followed me everywhere. It was like having a dog on a leash.

Joan Rivers

Do dogs wag their tails because they are happy or are they happy because they wag their tails?

Roba (Boule et Bill)

I'm not a guard dog! Defense dog? No more!... Attack dog? Even less!... So what?

Roba (Boule et Bill)

I do not understand, Mister Teacher, there is a total idiot who has imitated the cat's mewing and the dog thought it was you!

Roba (Boule et Bill)

If only I held the first dog that started to pick up balls!

Roba (Boule et Bill)

He had no penchant for barking dogs, wet dawn in the marshes and bleeding game meat.

David Robbins

From a dog's point of view his master is an elongated abnormally cunning dog.
Mabel L. Robinson

During the siege of Paris, the most distinguished women ate dog. It was hoped that it would inculcate in them the principles of loyalty. Not at all! They all claimed necklaces.
Henri de Rochefort

When they slammed the car door
He did not immediately understand.
He ran behind a long time
But the car was going too fast.
Jean Rochefort

If a picture wasn't doing very well, I'd put a puppy dog in it, always a mongrel, you know, never one of your thoroughbred puppies. And then I'd put a bandage on its foot... I liked it when I did it, but now I'm sick of it.
Norman Rockwell

He affected a deep contempt for dogs, because he thought they were subservient and groveling, and great respect for cats, because he thought they had a more open temper, and no less attachment.
Roderer

I start thinking about where my mom is or if my dogs have been fed.
Alex Rodriguez

I love a dog. He does nothing for political reasons.
Will Rogers

No man can be condemned for owning a dog. As long as he has a dog, he has a friend; and the poorer he gets, the better friend he has.
Will Rogers

The more I see of men, the more I admire dogs.
Jeanne-Marie Roland

What is best in man is the dog.
Gabrielle Rolin

Millionaire socialists, I have an idea that it is like dog turd. It must be a blessing.
Jules Romains

If dogs could talk, it would take a lot of fun out of owning one.
Andrew A. Rooney

The average dog is a nicer person than the average person.
Andrew A. Rooney

The quickest way to become an old dog is to stop learning new tricks.

John Rooney

You do not just attack me and my family, but now you include my little dog Fala. Your attacks do not offend me, but Fala is very sensitive to it. I have the right to express my indignation and opposition against your defamatory statements about my dog.
Franklin Delano Roosevelt

Nothing can look so well at someone crying as an old dog
Edmond Rostand

Dogs are getting bigger, according to a leading dog manufacturer.
Leo Calvin Rosten

Any man that hates dogs and babies can't be all that bad.
Leo Calvin Rosten

When you are a cat, you are a cat. When you are a cat you are not a dog.
Jacques Roubaud

The feigned charity of the rich man is for him nothing more than another luxury, he feeds the poor as he does dogs and horses.
Jean-Jacques Rousseau

The conquest of Khwarezm by Genghis Khan: we are talking about hundreds of thousands of victims, the killing of any living thing, including dogs and cats - but artisans and priests of all religions were saved,
Jean-Paul Roux

A cat is rarely enthusiastic. A dog is, too often. A man, too.
Claude Roy

Crazy love : only a dog or those with a simple soul can know, by the presence of the beloved, if they are to expect anything in return.
Jules Roy

That counts, even though it's a dog, someone who prefers you to the rest of the world.
Jules Roy

I wonder if other dogs think poodles are members of a weird religious cult.
Rita Rudner

My husband and I are either going to buy a dog or have a child. We can't decide whether to ruin our carpets or ruin our lives.
Rita Rudner

A timid dog barks more violently than it bites. Curtius Canis timidus vehementius latrat quam mordet
Quintus Curtius Rufus

Big change in l'Humanité: Pif the dog is now on page 31.

Laurent Ruquier

Delanoe is not about to do anything against dog turds on the sidewalks, as it's surely because he walked in one of them, his left foot first, that he ended up being the single candidate!

Laurent Ruquier

The pit-bull is a dog to whom, no sooner have you sent him the ball, you have to tell that he must bring back daddy's arm!

Laurent Ruquier

Enjoy the traffic jams during the weekend with your wife, the three children, the dog and the grandmother, Thanks to Renault, test on yourself the effect of aging in Space.

Laurent Ruquier

A dog cannot relate his autobiography; however eloquently he may bark, he cannot tell you that his parents were honest but poor.

Bertrand Russell

But, you might say, none of this shakes my belief that 2 and 2 is 4. You are quite right, except in marginal cases - and it is only in marginal cases that you are doubtful whether a certain animal is a dog or a certain length is less than a meter. Two must be two of something, and the proposition 2 and 2 is 4 is useless unless it can be applied. Two dogs and two dogs are certainly four dogs, but cases arise in which you are doubtful whether two of them are dogs. Well, at any rate there are four animals, you may say. But there are micro-organisms concerning which it is doubtful whether they are animals or plants. Well, then, living organisms, you say. But there are things of which it is doubtful whether they are living organisms or not. You will be driven into saying: Two entities and two entities are four entities. When you have told me what you mean by entity, we will resume the argument.

Bertrand Russell

Use kindness even to a malicious man: the best is to shut the dog's mouth with a mouthful.

Mocharrafoddin Saadi

No matter how little money and how few possessions you own, having a dog makes you rich.

Louis Sabin

It is not by a hazardous image that a Warrant is called a quarterdog, he keeps the world's most bleating flock, and the most amorphous.

Maurice Sachs

If we put hardened criminals back at school, it is as if at SPCA they had a hungry lion enter a cage of Chihuahuas.
Nicolas Sarkozi

He looked timid and the sniffing type, with a dog-like glance under his thick eyebrows.
Jean-Paul Sartre

The more I know men, the more I admire dogs.
Erik Satie

The word dog has never bitten anyone.
Ferdinand de Saussure

A cross-Setter, it is not reasonable having one in a flat.
Danny Saval

I once decided not to date a guy because he wasn't excited about meeting my dog. I mean, this was like not wanting to meet my mother.
Bonnie Schacter

It has everything of a dog but the loyal side.
Franklin Schaffner

Paris is the city where gutters are the cleanest in the world because dogs respect them.
Alain Schifres

I have suffered only two refusals, one from Michel Rocard and the second from the Chirac couple: it bothered them that the event took place in a gambling club. All the other masters were very proud that we were interested in their dogs.
Antoine Schneck

In Paris, in 1870, during the siege, all women ate dog. It was hoped that it would inculcate the principles of loyalty in the milky sex. Not at all! The dog produced an unexpected effect on these ladies; they claimed necklaces.
Aurélien Scholl

The French look at each other's buttonholes just as dogs sniff each other's you know what...
Aurélien Scholl

He who is cruel to animals cannot be a good man.
Arthur Schopenhauer

One could, indeed, wonder if there really are people who deserve esteem and sincere friendship. Anyway, I have more confidence in a good dog when it wags its tail, than in all these demonstrations and ways.

Arthur Schopenhauer

Nothing better reveals the ignorance of the world than claiming as proof of a man's merit and worth that he has many friends: as though men gave their friendship on the basis of value and merit! as if they were not similar to dogs who love the person who caresses them or just gives them bones, without caring for them any further.

Arthur Schopenhauer

Yesterday, I was a dog. Today I am a dog. To-morrow, I'll probably still be a dog. Damned! it's really difficult to get promotion!

Charles M. Schulz (Snoopy)

First you learn a new language, profanity; and second, you learn not to discipline your dogs when you're mad, and that's most of the time, when you're training dogs.

Lou Schultz

Do not make the mistake of treating your dogs like humans or they will treat you like dogs.

Martha Scott

Recollect that the Almighty, who gave us the dog as companion of our pleasures and our toils, hath invested him with a nature noble and incapable of deceit.

Sir Walter Scott

Let's take care of our style, it is our dog

Louis Scutenaire

I do not want to go to Denmark. I do not want to live in a country inhabited only by dogs... Nor in Beijing either, for that matter.

Patrick Sébastien

Adoption is often giving a home to one who is clean, affectionate, beautiful and does not pee on the carpet... It also applies to dogs.

Patrick Sébastien

Poker-playing dogs must imperatively keep their tails tied

Patrick Sébastien

Among God's creatures two, the dog and the guitar, have taken on all the sizes and all the shapes, in order not to be separated from man.

Andres Segovia

Clouseau: Does yer dewg bite?
Inn Keeper: No
Clouseau: Nice Doggy (bends down to pet a dachshund - it snarls and

bites him) I thought you said yer dewg did not bite!
Inn Keeper: Zat... iz not my dog!

Peter Sellers

What with our hooks, snares, nets, and dogs, we are at war with all living creatures, and nothing comes amiss but that which is either too cheap or too common; and all this is to gratify a fantastic palate.

Sénèque

The more I see men, the more I admire dogs.

Marquise de Sévigné

As for Jews, they don't like dogs. A dog, that bites you, that chases you, that barks at you. And it's been so long that the Jews have been bitten, chased or barked over that, finally, they prefer cats.

Joann Sfar (the Rabbi's Cat)

In Jewish tradition, the dog is a good pet because he is frank, opinionated, quick to endure suffering for the common good. While the cat, pff! You cannot trust a cat.

Joann Sfar (the Rabbi's Cat)

The Torah speaks more of humans than of cats or dogs.

Joann Sfar (the Rabbi's Cat)

And my poor fool is hanged! No, no, no life! Why should a dog, a horse, a rat, have life, And thou, no breath at all? Thou'lt come no more, Never, Never, Never, Never, Never!

William Shakespeare

First Witch: Thrice the brinded cat hath mewed.

Second Witch: Thrice, and once the hedge-pig whined.

Third Witch: Harpier cries "'Tis time, 'tis time."

First Witch: Round about the cauldron go;
In the poison'd entrails throw.
Toad, that under cold stone
Days and nights has thirty-one
Swelter'd venom sleeping got, Boil thou first i' the charmed pot.

ALL: Double, double toil and trouble;
Fire burn, and cauldron bubble.

Second Witch: Fillet of a fenny snake,
In the cauldron boil and bake;
Eye of newt and toe of frog,
Wool of bat and tongue of dog,

Adder's fork and blind-worm's sting,
Lizard's leg and owlet's wing,
For a charm of powerful trouble,
Like a hell-broth boil and bubble.

ALL: Double, double toil and trouble;
Fire burn, and cauldron bubble.

Third Witch: Scale of dragon, tooth of wolf,
Witches' mummy, maw and gulf
Of the ravin'd salt-sea shark,
Root of hemlock digg'd i' the dark,
Liver of blaspheming Jew,
Gall of goat, and slips of yew
Silver'd in the moon's eclipse,
Nose of Turk and Tartar's lips,
Finger of birth-strangled babe
Ditch-deliver'd by a drab,
Make the gruel thick, and slab:
Add thereto a tiger's chaudron,
For the ingredients of our cauldron.

ALL: Double, double toil and trouble;
Fire burn, and cauldron bubble.

Second Witch: Cool it with a baboon's blood,
Then the charm is firm and good.

William Shakespeare

I had rather be a dog, and bay at the moon,
Than such a Roman.

William Shakespeare

The cat will mew, and the dog will have his day.

William Shakespeare

I like a bit of a mongrel myself, whether it's a man or a dog. They're the best for every day.

George Bernard Shaw

If you eliminate smoking and gambling, you will be amazed to find that almost all of an Englishman's pleasures can be, and mostly are, shared by his dog.

George Bernard Shaw

Money will buy you a pretty good dog, but it won't buy the wag of his tail.

Henry Wheeler Shaw

Loyalty and jealousy are the greatness of dogs and the misfortune of saints.
Lao She

When you eat meat, the least you can do is to let the bone be gnawed at. There are always good-willed people to play the dog.
Lao She

My dog is half pit bull, half poodle. Not much of a watchdog, but a vicious gossip!
Craig Shoemaker

Every second that we refuse to love each other, a poor little baby dog sheds a new tear.
David Shore

This is the 21st century, we have flying cars, robot dogs and penicillin.
David Shore

I am a donkey, not a dog? If I were a dog, they 'd call me "The Dog", not "The Ass"!
Shrek

Oh, yeah, what are you gonna do? Release the dogs? Or the bees? Or the dogs with bees in their mouths and when they bark, they'll shoot bees at you?
Homer Simpsons

Man is an animal that makes bargains; no other animal does - one dog does not exchange a bone with another.
Adam Smith

Unless you're a lead dog, the scenery never changes.
Hannah Whitall Smith

Man is an animal that does business. A dog does not exchange his bones with another.
Sydney Smith

Even the mute dog barks at the end.
Alexandre Soljenitsyne

My dog can bark like a congressman, fetch like an aide, beg like a press secretary and play dead like a receptionist when the phone rings.
Gerald B H Solomon

You can wipe us out. But the children of the stars will never be dogs.
Somabulano

The awful thing to see a dog pissing! The awful thing to see a naked dog!

Baudeau de Somaize

The dog is the symbol of loyalty, but we have him on a leash.
Sövény

I'm not a big believer in such games as "bark like a chicken", "cackle like a dog"...
Stargate SG1

The more I see of men the more I like dogs.
Anne Louise Germaine de Stael

Dogs... I love their look of freedom, their way of living their fifteen years without any metaphysics.
Jules Stéfan

I am I because my little dog knows me
Gertrude Stein

I've seen a look in dogs' eyes, a quickly vanishing look of amazed contempt, and I am convinced that basically dogs think humans are nuts.
John Steinbeck

In the streets of New York between seven and nine in the morning you will see the slow procession of dog and owner proceeding from street to tree to hydrant to trash basket. They are apartment dogs. They are taken out twice a day, and, while it is a cliché, it is truly amazing how owner and dog resemble each other. They grow to walk alike and have the same set of heads.
John Steinbeck

On the Internet, nobody knows you're a dog.
Peter Steiner

Imagine believing in the control of inflation by curbing money supply! That is like deciding to stop your dog fouling the sidewalk by plugging up its rear end. It is highly unlikely to succeed, but if it does, it kills the hound.
Michael D. Stephens

You can give an order to a dog. To a cat, you can at most make a reasonable proposal.
Michael Stevens

If we value the pursuit of knowledge, we must be free to follow wherever that search may lead us. The free mind is no barking dog, to be tethered on a ten-foot chain.
Adlai E Stevenson Jr.

The cat, the rat, and Lovell the dog. All England is governed by a pig.
Robert Louis Stevenson

Dogs live with man as courtiers 'round a monarch steeped in the flattery of his notice... To push their favour in this world of pickings and caresses is, perhaps, the business of their lives.
Robert Louis Stevenson

You think those dogs will not be in heaven! I tell you they will be there long before any of us.
Robert Louis Stevenson

I loathe people who keep dogs. They are cowards who have not the guts to bite people themselves.
August Strindberg

You are a mystery in an enigma in a big ball of fur,
An irresistible magnet to every child and flea and burr.
Your nose is high-resolution while I live in a near-scentless fog
You run at high speed, while I just have to slog (but it's a good ol' slog)
So I just want to thank you for being my dog....
Richard Summerbell

The past, the future
Like twin dogs sniff around us.
Jules Supervielle

Bad company is like the dog that dirties most the people he loves best.
Jonathan Swift

Brutes find out where their talents lie;
A bear will not attempt to fly,
A foundered horse will oft debate
Before he tries a five- barred gate.
A dog by instinct turns aside
Who sees the ditch too deep and wide,
But man we find the only creature
Who, led by folly, combats nature;
Who, when she loudly cries-Forbear!
With obstinacy fixes there;
And whose genius least inclines,
Absurdly bends his whole designs.
Jonathan Swift

Every dog must have his day.
Jonathan Swift

I know Sir John will go, though he was sure it would rain cats and dogs.
Jonathan Swift

Following Emperor Nero's command, let the Christians be exterminated!:... they were made the subjects of sport; they were covered with the hides of wild beasts and worried to death by dogs, or nailed to crosses or set fire to, and when the day waned, burned to serve for the evening lights.

Publius Cornelius Tacite

Modern houses are so small we've had to train our dog to wag its tail up and down and not sideways.

Publius Cornelius Tacite

Breed not a savage dog, nor permit a shaky stairway.

Talmud

Rather be the tail of a lion than the head of a dog.

Talmud

The policy of the dead dog that follows the current.

André Tardieu

You know why dogs sniff buttocks? Well, just imagine that, when the Earth was ruled by dogs, they decided to hold a sort of congress to pass new laws. Then the dog who chaired the meeting said: "Listen, since we will remain several days in here, I propose, for hygiene reasons, we leave our arse holes in the cloakroom." All dogs approve, and presto! There they arse-hole off. But no sooner had the session begun, shuit! hop, there's a storm that rises and a real tornado shuit! All arse holes were mixed together. And there wasn't a single dog that was able to recognize his own. Since that time, they have always sniffed their buttocks. Then there's a chance that it will last until the end of the world.

Bertrand Tavernier

Dogs eat. Cats dine.

Ann Taylor

Some of my best leading men have been dogs and horses.

Elizabeth Taylor

The jinns can take a human or an animal form such as a cow, a scorpion, a snake, a bird... The black dog is the devil of dogs and jinn often appear in this form. They can also appear as a black cat because in fact black adds to the negative force of the devils.

Ibn Taymiya

For example, you'll get a picture of a moonlit night if you write that on the dam of the mill a piece of broken bottle flashed like a bright star and the black shadow of a dog or a wolf rolled by like a ball...

Anton Pavlovich Tchekhov

A starving dog has faith only in meat.
Anton Pavlovitch Tchekhov

A good man is ashamed even in front of a dog.
Anton Pavlovitch Tchekhov

He will hold thee, when his passion shall have spent its novel force, something better than his dog, a little dearer than his horse.
Lord Alfred Tennyson

Like a dog, he hunts in dreams.
Lord Alfred Tennyson

The dog gives the child the feeling of being useful and very appreciated.
Evelyne Terauni

The dog is a wonderful companion to whom children can relate all their woes. He accepts them as they are and don't judge them. It's an ally with whom a child finds solace when he has been scolded, baffled, or has got a bad grade at school.
Evelyne Torauni

Dogs, the foremost snobs in creation, are quick to notice the difference between a well-clad and a disreputable stranger.
Albert Payson Terhune

Should dogs have a harder tongue, they could speak.
Daniel Thibon

It is not because we do not like people that we must love dogs.
Hubert-Félix Thiéfaine

If dogs are not there, it is not heaven.
Elisabeth M. Thomas

As for the Pyramids, there is nothing to wonder at in them so much as the fact that so many men could be found degraded enough to spend their lives constructing a tomb for some ambitious booby, whom it would have been wiser and manlier to have drowned in the Nile, and then given his body to the dogs.
Henry David Thoreau

It often happens that a man is more humanely related to a cat or a dog than to any human being.
Henry David Thoreau

When a dog runs at you, whistle for him.
Henry David Thoreau

I prefer dogs to cats and all felines remind me of it at first glance - a sharp and unforgiving glance.
James Thurber

I have always thought of a dog lover as a dog that was in love with another dog.
James Thurber

If I have any beliefs about immortality, it is that certain dogs I have known will go to heaven, and very, very few persons.
James Thurber

The dog has seldom been successful in pulling man up to its level of sagacity, but man has frequently dragged the dog down to his.
James Thurber

When I see dogs say hello, I think that in every dog there is surely a proctologist who sleeps...
Patrick Timsit

Who loves a cat loves all cats. Who loves his dog does not love the others.
Roland Topor

Who eats the dog's kidneys distinguishes good from evil...
Roland Topor et Jean-Michel Ribes

- Ah! If, one day, thought the king, someone could love me for myself, without treachery, selfishness or lies.
The chaplain said:
- Take a dog.
Paul-Jean Toulet

Better - if you scream - with wolves than with dogs.
Paul-Jean Toulet

Dogs vie with women in giving themselves, faithfully. And if they do change, they change masters, but not bondages.
Paul-Jean Toulet

Man does not walk his dog, he is walked by his dog.
Michel Tournier

The cat seems to see it as a point of honour to be to be of no use at all, this does not prevent him from claiming a better place at home than the dog.
Michel Tournier

The more one gets to know men, the more one values dogs.
A Toussenel

America is a large, friendly dog in a very small room. Every time it wags its tail it knocks over a chair.
Arnold Joseph Toynbee

A hungry dog hunts best.
Lee Trevino

Children and dogs are as necessary to the welfare of the country as Wall Street and the railroads.
Harry S Truman

If you want a friend in Washington, take a dog.
Harry S. Truman

A dog is not a good dog because he barks well. A man is not wise because he speaks well. It is not enough to strive to be great. Nor to be virtuous.
Tchouang-Tseu

Dogs' lives are too short, their only fault really.
Agnes Sligh Turnbull

By what right has the dog come to be regarded as a noble animal? The more brutal and cruel and unjust you are to him the more your fawning and adoring slave he becomes; whereas, if you shamefully misuse a cat once, she will always maintain a dignified reserve towards you afterward- you will never get her full confidence again.
Mark Twain

Every time you stop a school, you will have to build a jail. What you gain at one end you lose at the other. It's like feeding a dog on his own tail. It won't fatten the dog.
Mark Twain

Heaven goes by favour. If it went by merit, your dog would go in and you would stay out.
Mark Twain

It's not the size of the dog in the fight, it's the size of the fight in the dog.
Mark Twain

If you pick up a starving dog and make him prosperous, he will not bite you; that is the principal difference between a dog and a man.
Mark Twain

In an hour I taught a cat and a dog to be friends. I put them in a cage. In another hour I taught them to be friends with a rabbit. In the course of two days I was able to add a fox, a goose, a squirrel and some doves. Finally, a monkey. They lived together in peace; even affectionately.

The dog is a gentleman; I hope to go to his heaven, not man's.
Mark Twain

When a man's dog turns against him, it is time for his wife to pack her trunk and go home to mamma.
Mark Twain

The dog is the only one who loves you more than he loves himself.
Fritz Von Unrub

A garden is not merely a piece of nature fenced in near the house, like a wolf chained at the back door; but nature cultivated and trained like a dog tamed and trained for human ends.
Abram Linwood Urban

We believe that a dog's life is approximately one seventh of that of a man. But a president does not even deserve a dog's life.
Peter Ustinov

Cats are smarter than dogs. You cannot get eight cats to pull a sled through snow.
Jeff Valdez

The motto of the cat: no matter what you did, still try to pretend that it is the fault of the dog.
Jeff Valdez

Today my aunt caught her dog eating the parrot that he had been given to look after. As punishment, she put what was left of the parrot in the freezer. And now, she hits him with the frozen bird, shouting: "Look what you did!".
VDM (Collectif)

An old dog must not bark anymore, as long as he can no longer bite.
Peter Veres

What do I see? A kind of fellow beating up with a vengeance an unfortunate yellow dog who howled heart-breakingly.
Louis Verneuil

The one absolutely unselfish friend that man can have in this selfish world, the one that never deserts him, the one that never proves ungrateful or treacherous, is his dog....He will kiss the hand that has no food to offer; he will lick the wounds and sores that have encountered the roughness of the world... When all other friends desert, he remains.
George G Vest

What's better in man is the dog.
Alexandre Vialatte

A good dog is better than two kilos of rats.
Boris Vian

If you want to live, love and die regretted, profit by the example of Dash.
Queen Victoria

Do not lead your dog on a leash if you want him to be attached.
André Villemetz

An old servant opened the door, escorted by a huge red-haired dachshund, who must add to his house functions as a watchdog that of strangler of Messrs the rats.
Villiers de l'Isle-Adam

Dog without a muzzle, woman without a distaff, man without a knife make a sad world of little sense.
Henri Vincenot

Even though Spaniels have the reputation of being the best of friends, they can't compare with you.
Voltaire

If you want news about our armies, the Champagne regiment fought like a lion and was beaten like a dog.
Voltaire

Men in general are like dogs that howl when they hear other dogs howling in the distance.
Voltaire

You own a dog but you feed a cat.
Jenny de Vries

Let dogs delight in barking and biting For God hath made them so
Let bears and lions growl and fight for it is their nature, too.
Isaac Watts

It takes a strong- minded human to appreciate a string-minded dog!
Mary Webber

There are guide dogs but never guide cats.
Bernard Werber

There are tramp dogs but no tramp cats. When a cat sees that his master can no longer afford to feed him, he abandons him to find another more fortunate. As for dogs, they are what they are but they remain faithful to their master, even if poor, until death.

Bernard Werber

Cowardly dogs bark loudest.
John Webster

My dog is worried about the economy because Alpo is up to 99 cents a can. That's almost $7.00 in dog money.
Joe Weinstein

You know the secrets of the queen? Did she drop her dogs in your footsteps?
Margaret Weis

The cat, which is a solitary beast, is single-minded and goes his way alone; but the dog, like his master, is confused in his mind.
H.G. Wells

A reasonable amount of fleas is good for a dog; it keeps him from brooding over being a dog.
Edward Noyes Westcott

My little old dog, a heartbeat at my feet.
Edith Wharton

A really companionable and indispensable dog is an accident of nature. You can't get it by breeding for it, and you can't buy it with money. It just happens along.
E B White

If a dog jumps in your lap, it is because he is fond of you; but if a cat does the same thing, it is because your lap is warmer.
Alfred North Whitehead

Classical conditioning (also Pavlovian or respondent conditioning, Pavlovian reinforcement) is a form of associative learning that was first demonstrated by Ivan Pavlov. The typical procedure for inducing classical conditioning involves presentations of a neutral stimulus along with a stimulus of some significance. The neutral stimulus could be any event that does not result in an overt behavioral response from the organism under investigation. Pavlov referred to this as a conditioned stimulus (CS). Conversely, presentation of the significant stimulus necessarily evokes an innate, often reflexive, response. Pavlov called these the unconditioned stimulus (US) and the unconditioned response (UR), respectively. If the CS and the US are repeatedly paired, eventually the two stimuli become associated and the organism begins to produce a behavioral response to the CS. Pavlov called this the conditioned response (CR).

Popular forms of classical conditioning that are used to study neural structures and functions that underlie learning and memory include fear conditioning, eye blink conditioning, and the foot contraction conditioning of Hermissenda crassicornis.

The original and most famous example of classical conditioning involved the salivary conditioning of Pavlov's dogs. During his research on the physiology of digestion in dogs, Pavlov noticed that, rather than simply salivating in the presence of meat powder (an innate response to food that he called the unconditioned response), the dogs began to salivate in the presence of the lab technician who normally fed them. Pavlov called these psychic secretions. From this observation he predicted that, if a particular stimulus in the dog's surroundings were present when the dog was presented with meat powder, then this stimulus would become associated with food and cause salivation on its own. In his initial experiment, Pavlov used a metronome to call the dogs to their food and, after a few repetitions, the dogs started to salivate in response to the metronome. Thus, a neutral stimulus (metronome) became a conditioned stimulus (CS) as a result of consistent pairing with the unconditioned stimulus (US - meat powder in this example). Pavlov referred to this learned relationship as a conditional reflex (now called conditioned response).
Wikipedia

Old dogs, like old shoes, are comfortable. They might be a bit out of shape and a little worn around the edges, but they fit well.
Bonnie Wilcox

Many who have spent a lifetime in it can tell us less of love than the child that lost a dog yesterday.
Thornton Wilder

There is no psychiatrist in the world like a puppy licking your face.
Ben Williams

I have always liked bird dogs better than kennel-fed dogs myself, you know, one that will get out and hunt for food rather than sit on his fanny and yell.
Charles Erwin Wilson

He may look just the same to you, and he may be just as fine, But the next-door dog is the next-door dog, and mine - is - mine.
Dixie Wilson

If you ain't the lead dog, the scenery never changes.
Edmund Wilson

Any dog may bite once, but in the case of a dog who does not stop biting, we adopt a different view.

Harold Wilson

The final war will be between Pavlov's dog and Schrödinger's cat.

Robert Anton Wilson

If a dog will not come to you after he has looked you in the face, you ought to go home and examine your conscience.

Woodrow Wilson

The trouble with cats is that they've got no tact.

P. G. Wodehouse

If it were a dog, it would have bitten you already. (Meaning: said to someone who is looking for something which is right under his nose).

Twents Woordenbook

I bought a dog the other day... I named him Stay. It's fun to call him... Come here, Stay! Come here, Stay! He went insane. Now he just ignores me and keeps typing.

Steven Wright

I put contact lenses in my dog's eyes. They had little pictures of cats on them. Then I took one out and he ran around in circles.

Steven Wright

I took my dog for a walk... all the way from New York to Florida... I said to him There now you're done.

Steven Wright

I spilled spot remover on my dog. Now he's gone.

Steven Wright

My dog is an East German Shepherd.

Steven Wright

The other day, I was walking my dog around my building... on the ledge. Some people are afraid of heights. Not me, I'm afraid of widths.

Steven Wright

There are only two species on earth that are able sometimes to give themselves entirely to comradeship through the eyes: man and the dog.

Jean-Michel Wyl

- There are still 650 Parisians this year who ended up in hospital after slipping on dog turds.
- They should walk in the gutter!

Jean Yanne

The Promenade des Anglais in Nice, it is the only place where dogs are slipping on elders' turds.
Jean Yanne

Cats are oppressed, dogs terrify them, landladies starve them, boys stone them, everybody speaks of them with contempt.
William Butler Yeats

What shall I do with this absurdity?
O heart, O troubled heart-this caricature,
Decrepit age that has been tied to me
As to a dog's tail?
William Butler Yeats

Men are like dogs, you must rotate the sugar and the slap!
Ariel Zeitoun

A rough-haired fawn sheepdog, curled up near the hearth, looked at the poultry with a dreaming eye.
Michel Zévaco

Suddenly, the red dog looked up and suddenly stood up, sniffing. He gave a yelp when he was mad with joy, then wagging his stumpy tail frenzily, rushed like an arrow into the room.
Michel Zévaco

The long gloomy bark of the dog punctuated the defeat of his master.
Michel Zévaco

A dog is not considered a good dog because he is a good barker. A man is not considered a good man because he is a good speaker.
Zhuangzi

It is the way of a dog that, if hit by a stone, he bites a fellow dog.
The Zohar

He has entered into my life to such a point that it is beyond words.
Emile Zola

I had a small dog, a griffon of the smallest species, named Fanfan. One day at the Dog Show, in Cours la Reine, I saw him in a cage in the company of a big cat. And he looked at me with eyes so full of tenderness, I told the salesman to release him from that cage for a while. Then, once on the ground, he began to walk like a dog on wheels. So excited I was, I purchased it.
Emile Zola

I want to tell you that one of the cruellest hours, amid the dreadful hours I've spent, was when I learned the sudden death away from me, of the faithful little companion, who for nine years had never left me.
Emile Zola

It has been said that animals are replacing children for old maids for whom devotion is not enough. And this is not true, love of animals continues, does not give in to mother love, when he awakes in a woman. This fondness is very special, it is not affected by other feelings, and it does not break them.
Emile Zola

The love of animals is, like all great sentiments, ridiculous and delicious, full of madness and sweetness, capable of true extravagance as well as of the wisest, strongest will.
Emile Zola

The truth is that everybody loves animals but there are people who do not know that they love them. Can you imagine nature without animals, a prairie without insects, a forest without birds, mountains and plains without living beings? Imagine for a moment man alone and at once what an immense desert, what silence, what stillness, what horrible sadness!
Émile Zola

There are kennels for dogs which are closed on one side; ask for such a one, so he does not freeze. Finally, try to install him for the better. Strictly speaking, offer a two-franc piece to the driver and ask him what could be done to protect the poor animal from inflammation of the lungs.
Emile Zola

You know, I'm not a bitch. I do not put my feet up when I'm whistled!
Emile Zola

SUMMARY

PREFACE	9
CAT, DOG AND MAN: THE LEGEND OF THE ORIGINS	11
MY CAT TOLD ME	15
Inscriptions on the Royal Tombs at Thebes	15
Anonymous quotations	16
Quotations from authors	22
THE MYSTERY CAT	133
MY DOG TOLD ME	135
Anonymous quotations	135
Quotations from authors	142

Read our illustrated quotations in

Mot à mau
Mau Mews
Didier Hallépée
Carrefour du Net publisher

bilingual edition

Mot à Mau
Les pensées du chat mau

Didier Hallépée

Animaux

Read our illustrated quotations in

Pensées Royales Canines
King Barks
Didier Hallépée
Carrefour du Net publisher

bilingual edition

PENSÉES ROYALES CANINES
LES PENSÉES DU KING CHARLES

DIDIER HALLÉPÉE

COLLECTION ARC-EN-CIEL
ANIMAUX

The cat and the dog have been occupying a prominent place in our homes and at our sides for many years. It is normal to come across them at any time in our literature or when visiting a website. Sometimes they occupy the central place and there are many books that have been devoted to them, sometimes by writers less well known than their companions... Other times, they are just making the scene more lively, more truthful, because without them, where would be the soul of our homes?

Through these quotes, you will first travel in time, across regions religions and cultures: the Bible, Einstein, Mahomet, Queen Elisabeth II, Shakespeare, Agatha Christie and many others.

This little journey into the heart of wisdom or in the company of famous personalities will give you all the delights that our fourlegged friends deserve. And at the heart of all these treasures, I'm sure you will find valuable thoughts to illuminate your every day.

His life in a familly of Egyptian Maus and King Charles Spaniels made him sensitive to the deepness of the thoughts of our favorite 4-legs. **Didier HALLÉPÉE** shares with us the many quotations he met in the over ten thousand books he could read.

www.ingramcontent.com/pod-product-compliance
Lightning Source LLC
Chambersburg PA
CBHW071432150426
43191CB00008B/1107